RUBIES & ROSES

1. *(Frontispiece)* CORAL-ROSE TREE. This collector's item shows the influence of flowers on the artists of today. The roses are made of coral and the leaves of jade; the 14-carat gold stems are set in chips of malachite. (Courtesy of Cartier, Inc., New York.)

Rubies & Roses

GEMS PORTRAYED IN FLOWERS

by PEGGY FEASEY

CHARLES E. TUTTLE COMPANY
Rutland, Vermont & Tokyo, Japan

Representatives

For Continental Europe:
BOXERBOOKS, INC., *Zurich*
For the British Isles:
PRENTICE-HALL INTERNATIONAL, INC., *London*
For Australasia:
PAUL FLESCH & CO., PTY. LTD., *Melbourne*
For Canada:
M. G. HURTIG LTD., *Edmonton*

Published by the Charles E. Tuttle Company, Inc.
of Rutland, Vermont & Tokyo, Japan
with editorial offices at
Suido 1-chome, 2-6, Bunkyo-ku, Tokyo

Copyright in Japan, 1969
by Charles E. Tuttle Co., Inc.

Library of Congress Catalog Card No. 72-83077
Standard Book No. 8048 0507-5

First printing, 1970

Book design & typography by F. Sakade
Layout of plates by H. Doki
PRINTED IN JAPAN

To the two men in my life both named

ERIC

I lovingly dedicate this book

TABLE OF CONTENTS

LIST OF ILLUSTRATIONS

FOREWORD

BY EMMA HODKINSON CYPHERS

A FLOWER arranger's desire to extend his art beyond mere decoration for the home is always a major challenge. Through the years I have watched Peggy Feasey's delight in gem stones as well as in flowers, so it is not surprising to find that she has met the challenge with a fascinating approach to the subject of flower arrangement—the harmony that exists between flowers and gems.

For mankind, there is a close relationship between these products of nature, even though they differ greatly in substance. Man has regarded with awe certain stones as he has certain plants, for like the most ordinary flower of the field the commonest gem stone is a miracle of God's creation. The human passion for both has existed from earliest times, when stones and flowers were held sacred, valued for their symbolism, and were employed in religious ritual. Among the many ancient uses, both jewels and flowers served as self-adornment, a practice that endures today.

One's bias in the direction of a given subject invariably indicates ability to excel therein and indeed this is true of the author of this unique book. Mrs. Feasey has not merely acquired information; she experienced and enjoyed research, discovery, and collecting to such an extent that they spurred her to achievement in the lecture field. This volume is the result of the longing for greater knowledge and more detailed information that has stimulated so many of her listeners.

The author has not concerned herself with theoretical and mechanical instruction in the art of flower arrangement. Rather, she instills in her readers an awareness of the beauty and perfection of flowers and stones. By probing aesthetic sensitivity and imagination, she enables her readers to interpret the essence of precious and semiprecious stones through the medium of plant material. She sometimes combines flowers or foliage with a stone in the rough state, sometimes with stones cut and polished; sometimes she captures the character of a specific gem with nothing other than a discriminating selection of plant material.

As Mrs. Feasey explains, her text considers "a whole family of beautiful and enduring gems," beginning with the diamond as "king of precious stones" and ending with the pearl as "queen of gems." Particularly appealing are the entertaining historical facts and legendary accounts with which Mrs. Feasey spices her text. In this sincere and exciting work, the written word accompanied by inspiring plates cannot fail to enrich the outlook of flower arrangers and stimulate the pleasures of reflection, study and, above all, vision.

PREFACE

HE DECISION to write this book grew from the warm and enthusiastic reception given to my lectures relating flowers to gems. In the hour or hour and a half usually allotted me, I consistently felt a lack of time in which to do justice to the flower compositions. It was certainly not enough time for the fascinating stories of gems; too much had to be left unsaid.

Nature's dewdrops glittering in the sunlight and her insects of iridescent coloring are as attractive in color and perfect in form as any gem cut by the lapidary's skillful hand, but regrettably their beauty is fleeting. The memory of the beauty of nature's flowers may remain with us longer, but a flower is fragile and transient—all too quickly gone. The beauty of a jewel, on the other hand, is with us always, for natural gems withstand the ravages of time.

According to Persian legend, when God created the world He made no useless things such as gold, silver, or precious stones. Satan, always eager to cause evil, kept close watch to discern the passions of the human mind and heart. Perceiving that Eve loved the many-colored flowers in the Garden of Eden, he undertook to imitate their beauty and produced colored stones and diamonds. Evil? Useless? Indeed not! Just as surely as God blessed mankind with birds to delight the ear and with flowers to attract the eye, so He has blessed humanity with colorful stones to lift man's spirit.

I never cease to wonder at the magnificence which lies in our world of living. So much beauty is manifested in transient flowers and enduring, sparkling gems—especially when they are artfully combined. Too often the inherent beauty is only casually observed. It is my sincere hope that this volume will enrich and enhance the reader's feeling for color and texture, both in gems and flowers. With these two marvels of nature always available for your enjoyment, may you drink deeply of their beauty. With this in mind, then, recall the majesty of a perfectly formed lily as you contemplate the iridescence of a pearl necklace, and think of the textured loveliness of rose quartz as you study the silky threads of pink mimosa.

In all things there must be contrast, just as there is similarity. So enjoy the flower for its fragility, knowing it is here for but a short time. Enjoy precious stones, for by contrast they are evidence of the long and lasting beauty of our world. The purpose of this volume is to show the relationship between these beauties of nature—gems and flowers—and to stimulate you, the reader, to enlarge your vision and broaden your imagination.

For the sheer beauty and feeling of exaltation which lavish color will evoke, jewels in brilliantly executed designs cannot fail to instill a great love for antiquity. After all, what is of greater age than these flower colors from the depths of the earth? What is more needed in our world today than evidence of the beautiful and enduring? What touches our responsive thoughts and brings us again to the beauty of today more certainly and surely than fragile but long-remembered flowers? "The fragrance of antiquity lasts forever," goes an old Chinese saying.

I would like to add a note regarding the terminology. For many years the National Council of State Garden Clubs drew a distinction between flower arrangements and compositions in their club-sponsored flower shows. An arrangement was a design using only plant materials, freshly cut or in combination with dried plant materials; a composition, on the other hand, was a design in which a figurine, rocks, stones, or other accessories were incorporated into the design. This became most confusing, especially to the novice, and so the decision to eliminate the difference in terminology was made. In flower shows today, all designs, whether or not they use accessories, are acceptable. However, old habits are hard to unlearn, and I still prefer to classify a design according to the original distinction made by the National Council of State Garden Clubs. I have consistently referred to a design as an arrangement or a composition depending on whether or not I have used the subject stone or stones.

*   *   *

Without the encouragement of my dear friend, Emma Hodkinson Cyphers, this book would have remained only a thought. My daughter Janet, although entangled in blueprints and the almost insurmountable problems of building a hillside home, found time to proofread this manuscript. Two florists, Lou Bevacqua and Arthur Abrahamson, proved to be wonderful friends in their untiring efforts to find exactly the right flowers and leaves needed for interpretations. Clifton O. Stetson, managing director of Cartier, Inc., New York, kindly cooperated in supplying the transparency of the coral-rose tree (Frontispiece). Mrs. William Orvis and Mrs. Paul King, both of whom are neighbors and Garden Club members, gave generously from their gardens when the need arose.

Grateful acknowledgment is made to the American Museum of Natural History; N. W. Ayer and Son, Ltd.; De Beers Consolidated Mines, Ltd.; the Montclair Art Museum; and Ward's Natural Science Establishment for granting permission to reproduce many of the plates in this book. I would also like to thank the following photographers for allowing their work to be included: Floyd Getsinger, D. A. Murray, Fran Ortiz, Mary Alice and Jack Roche, William Sevecke, and Miki Takagi.

Finally, I am grateful to the various publishers for allowing me to quote from the works cited: Arthur Barker Ltd., *The Book of Necklaces* by Sah Oved, London, 1953; Blackie & Son, *Diamonds and Precious Stones* by Louis Dieulafait,

London, 1874; and David McKay Co., *Mogok, the Valley of Rubies* by Joseph Kessel, New York, 1960.

To these and others who have helped in so many ways I acknowledge a debt of gratitude.

—PEGGY FEASEY

EVER SINCE the first man could see beauty in simple things, visual experiences have been a part of forming our background. The first pebble picked up by primitive man—pretty in color, smooth in texture, and interesting in form—became the decorative stone for his mate. Wild flowers growing at the entrance to his cave became his first acknowledgment of beauty. Surely man's appreciation of beauty had its beginning in this fashion, and as time passed his experiences in visual and audible form were extended.

To paraphrase an axiom, curiosity became the mother of imagination. This led man onward; it led him to discover and identify with the familiar. Curiosity was always a driving force, just as it is today. Our minds reach for parallels because they fit comfortably into our thinking. But we should not stop here; we should allow our imaginations to develop. Imagination is a faculty of the mind and is responsible for thoughts running ahead and then fastening onto a like pattern far beyond the thought which first gave it impetus. It may then be called "inspiration," and many are the factors influencing it. Everyone has some degree of imagination, and it can be easily utilized. With a perceptive eye and an appreciation for beauty in whatever medium is used, expression of the inner self may be given.

True creativeness is never mundane, nor is it static, for inspiration is the result of individual reactions. Spiritual perceptiveness varies in each of us, and the development of our inspirations depends upon how we can best express ourselves. In flower arrangement we find satisfaction in working with something alive, something texturally pleasant and certainly most gratifying to the eye.

The beauty of flowers and leaves has strong influence on the jeweler's art, as well as on that of painters, sculptors, architects, and ceramists. When the art of flower arranging became formalized, the resultant beauty of combined textures and colors was clearly evident. In Japan the art flourished, for the Japanese in particular love flowers. Because of their love of nature they used stones with beauty of form and color in their floral designs as an integral part of their creations. A number of schools were formed which emphasized this use together with grasses, water plants, or whatever suited the type of stone used. Branches, blossoms, and stones depicted mountain scenes. Water plants, flowers, and materials which grow naturally at the water's edge were used to show the beauty of rocks found in streams. In this way their creations were completed, using stones as an integral part of the design.

There is, however, another approach to the use of stones in flower arranging. Study of the stone itself fosters inspiration. In the flower-arrangement medium, color and texture become important elements in the design. It is astonishing how many flowers, leaves, and branches bear strong resemblance to gems and semiprecious stones.

Inspiration comes to us in many ways because our imagination and the need to associate with the familiar in our thoughts are very demanding. Just as the eye is constructed so that it calls for completion of the color spectrum for visual satisfaction, so does the imagination reach out and seek images of familiarity. Allowing all the senses to gather experience widens our scope of mental exercise. Imagination runs a parallel course with these experiences, and inspiration comes into being. Does not music touch chords of inner response, just as does the sight of a beautiful form? Inspired in this manner, creativeness follows. Associated ideas will furnish the basis for creativity and expression of what is felt.

For instance, a mood or feeling may be expressed when jealousy is the subject. Does your mind not immediately conjure up green for expressing this mood? Why? Because the familiar is always demanded by the mind, and our minds have been conditioned to link green with envy.

The individual personalities of flowers can provide inspiration. Pansies seem naïve in spirit, smiling faces expressing their informal bloom. "Shy and modest" describe the violet, a child of the woodland, to perfection. The lilac is a true friend. The camellia is beautiful but unapproachable, its fragrance that of personality. A gardenia rushes warmly to greet you, while the rose remains aloof. Carnations seem to be asking where the gentlemen are, and peonies keep their enigmatic faces toward you, exuding the fragrance of old incense. Wild flowers are children of the woods, not sophisticated enough to be invited in to tea; yet there is dignity here, too, as tall cypripedia and pink lady's slippers watch over the behavior of other little wildlings. The hemerocallis is a jealous personality; petunias are dainty and youthful. While there is laughter in the beautiful face of the buttercup, gravity is etched in the hollyhock. These are but impressions; perhaps you, too, are subject to similar fantasies.

Music is another source of inspiration. Compositions written for the serious music of concerts, when interpreted in flower arrangement, call for use of strong colors and determined line. Stringed instruments suggest lighter values, pale hues such as yellow roses for the "Third Man Theme," for instance.

Visually there are many sources of inspiration. When I saw for the first time the painting by W. Y. Stamper called "The Perfume Counter," my imagination flew to the colored flowers which would match the well-defined bars of color in the painting, and immediately the inspiration was born to use the most fragrant of flowers—strongly scented gardenias, delicate peonies, delightful lilacs, and fragrant roses: association of ideas and imagination had become inspiration.

Textural qualities too can be a source of delight, such as those found in a mineral called ulexite. A perfect specimen is rare, but there is one in the Mineral Museum in Phoenix,

Arizona. Had nature set out deliberately to make in mineral form an exact duplicate of the delicate fairylike pattern of dandelion flowers gone to seed or the formation of a patch of white rabbit fur, the result could not have been achieved any more successfully. Ulexite is staggering in its beauty and perfection. Each tiny white thread is firmly held in place, glinting very slightly; each filament stands upright as in the seed head of dandelion. Source of inspiration? Ah, yes.

These qualities of beauty, in whatever form they are found, may be the basis for inspired designs. The study of stones, minerals, and the unusual formations of nature present a challenge, and an exciting one at that!

This volume begins with the diamond, the "King of precious stones," and ends with the pearl, the "Queen of gems." In between these is a whole world of stones and flowers of most compatible characteristics. There are many other beautiful polished and rough stones, but you must let your imagination carry you along when you view them. The school of cubist painters might well have taken its inspiration for overlapping planes and geometric surfaces from the mineral called wulfenite.

Inspiration may come from a mood. Who is immune to the awe stirred within one when entering the "Avenue of the Giants" in the redwood forests of California and Oregon? Who can remain aloof when stained glass windows in cathedrals and churches call forth an immediate emotional and spiritual response? In Palm Beach, Florida, a church called Bethesda-by-the-Sea has a stained glass window above the altar which is strongly reminiscent of the Harlequin Prince opal, a magnificent stone with strong green-and-blue lights. What a beautiful flower arrangement may be the result of allowing imagination to dictate and inspiration to create!

Man holds in his palm the gems which were un-considered minerals in the ground, and feasts his eyes on their intense color which lay hidden in the darkness of the earth. . . . They were created, as man was created, not alone for himself or his own delight—yet they need him to release their potential wonder. And he needs them, too, that he may, in all humility, seek to add to loveliness. For, forever and forever, the search for beauty will go on, since it is but the intensity of man's desire to be laid close to the bosom of God.

—Sah Oved

GEMS ARE
PRECIOUS STONES

EM STONES occupy a place unique in one's feelings; they exert a mysterious pull on human emotions. As one contemplates the mystery of eternity within their depths, one cannot help but discover a kind of microcosm filled with surprises and delights.

DEFINITION OF GEMS

What is a gem? The word comes from the Latin *gemma,* meaning bud. The lowly and obscure bud on the branch eventually grows into a blossom; from the dull and unattractive lump of mineral the scintillating, sparkling gem is wrought. So the parallel with plant life has begun: all gems are stones, whether mineral or inorganic in composition. Nature combines ores and metals with minerals which result in gems (precious stones) and semiprecious stones. Classification is difficult because the families of minerals overlap to a great degree; combinations of minerals are found in many stones. Except for the diamond, no stone is of a pure, single mineral content.

Since there are already many books on the composition of stones, I shall not go deeply into the subject. However, I will touch briefly on it where it affects the selection of plant material in the interpretation of a stone through the medium of flower arrangement.

Only four stones are considered precious: diamond, emerald, ruby, and sapphire. The United States Customs regulations identify only these as precious stones, and this designation has world-wide acceptance. Because these stones are rare, they are considered to be gems.

Beauty, hardness, purity, rarity, and size determine the value of all precious stones. A standard scale of hardness known as Mohs' scale has long been established. It is used to determine the genuineness of a stone, although other tests are also employed.

Diamond is the hardest substance known to man. The established standard of hardness assigned to it is ten. The ruby and the sapphire "cut in," as gemologists say, at slightly less than nine on the scale; the emerald at eight. Stones lower on the hardness scale are referred to as semiprecious. Amethyst and topaz are rated at about seven, but surely if beauty were the criteria, this quality would entitle them to the rating of gems. Lack of hardness and rarity, however, preclude this possibility.

Semiprecious stones, such as sardonyx, crystal, aventurine, and agate, are in more or less plentiful supply and are therefore not considered rare. They also are rated lower on Mohs' scale of hardness than are the precious stones. Besides this, semiprecious stones are more easily recognized. Therefore, any stone of this classification, being more common, is not frequently imitated; it seldom needs testing and certification by expert gemologists. These stones have characteristics which render them readily recognizable, and thus the need to be sure of their genuineness diminishes.

In attempting to interpret stones in flower arrangements, we have a textural problem and one which is greatly magnified in the case of gems with great reflective and transparent qualities. The very quality of brilliance which we love so much in gems defeats us when we seek it in flowers.

While the clear and transparent stones present an exciting challenge, the opaque stones are relatively easy to interpret with plant materials, and with few exceptions a remarkably close approximation can be made. Concerning the descriptions of plant materials in the arrangements that accompany the text on individual stones, you will see a remarkable parallel in texture and color between flowers and stones.

LUSTER AND BRILLIANCE

Precious stones have luster, sparkle, and flashing light with a power to enchant and inspire. Within their luminous depths is a clear transparency which gives us a vista of eternity.

Luster is to a gem what texture is to a flower. Brilliance, intensity of hue and a reflective quality give a stone great beauty. Flowers have a living, transient quality, while stones are hard and static. As texture controls the intensity of color to a marked degree, so does light affect the quality of the hue both in stones and flowers. The smooth, satiny sheen of a rose may be compared to the translucency of the moonstone or the pearl. Tiny flowers of blue lobelia, when clustered, display an intense blue; their centers of white dots give the effect of sparkle, heightening the brightness of a color similar to the sapphire. The *Lobelia cardinalis* possesses the same quality of brightness, and when individual blossoms are clustered its red hue is greatly intensified, with the tiny white centers adding a sparkle similar to that of a ruby. One might argue, "Who has enough cardinal flower to cluster in this fashion? It is so rare!" True, but isn't the ruby also rare?

Adding to the effectiveness of the color is luster, which is a radiance all its own. Gems, such as the ruby, sapphire, emerald, and diamond, have this very distinguishing feature. Their luster adds a depth of indescribable beauty.

Hybrids in flowers are the definite result of an intentional comingling of characteristics, but not so in the mineral world. Here, character is the result of nature's powerful forces that are never controllable: stones are as nature formed them. A horticulturist can tell by visual characteristics the family or genus to which a plant belongs. A gemologist, on the other hand, must avoid hasty judgment because of the many likenesses in the mineral world. For instance, chrysolite, peridot, olivine, green garnet, chlorospinel, and tourmaline present to the casual observer the same color and appearance and so are easily confused. Sometimes exhaustive tests are required to differentiate between them.

TEXTURE AND LIGHT

Color is greatly affected by texture. Pigment colors (those such as paint applied to a surface and those shown in color charts) are of the same texture. With stones, however, qualities of transparency and opaqueness enter into the problem; stones have elements of depth and construction which control light rays to a marked degree.

As light enters a stone, it is transformed into minute bands of color, since all hues of the spectrum are contained in white light. Some of the colors in light are absorbed or destroyed within the stone. Others are reflected and manifested to the human eye as the "mother" color of the stone. This reflection is typical of all transparent stones.

Among transparent or clear stones, diamonds alone have the remarkable ability to reflect all the color in the light that strikes them. As we will learn in our study of this particular gem, it reflects these colors many times over.

Light reflected from a shiny surface is termed "advancing" light. An example of such a surface in the plant world is the shiny green, waxlike leaf of the southern magnolia. The brown velvety texture of its underside, however, is not as reflective; light striking it is partially absorbed. The surface, therefore, has a dull, matte appearance. With stones it is the same: a shiny clear emerald reflects a brilliant, intensified green hue comparable to a shiny green leaf, while a satiny, opaque stone such as aventurine appears less bright. Because of the texture of aventurine, light on it produces an effect nearer to the matte surface of a geranium or nasturtium leaf.

In discussing amber, for instance, it will be brought out that this "stone," composed of what was once the sap of a tree, has a matte finish. It does not reflect light to the same degree as does a true stone, even one that is opaque. Its softer content gives it a velvety quality, dull rather than lustrous. Dull, too, is a velvety-surfaced leaf, or the center of such flowers as the black-eyed susan and the anemone.

Glyptic art, the art of carving or engraving on gems, was practiced as far back as 4000 B.C. The hardness and durable quality of stone has been responsible for its long preservation, and in many cases we are able to appreciate such work in its original state. Painting, sculpture, and architecture have all been seriously affected by the ravages of time, but not so with glyptic art. A gem engraving of exquisite minuteness and accuracy of detail often possesses the nobility and dignity of a bronze or marble sculpture, yet the work may be confined to the space of less than half a square inch.

INFLUENCE OF FLORAL AND PLANT FORMS
(FROM 4000 B.C. TO THE PRESENT)

Chenhu-Daro was an ancient town on the banks of the Indus River and is well known to students of archaeology and ancient history. Many highly skilled goldsmiths and silver-smiths (as well as ingenious toy makers) were among its inhabitants. The little community was a peaceful one, and its people had an intense love of agriculture and plant life. As the Indus River rolled down to the Arabian Sea, the people of Chenhu-Daro watched by the river banks while sheep-skin squares were placed in the stream-bed to catch deposits of fine gold as the water flowed over the fleece. At the end of the day, many gentle faces peering from under strange, baglike caps watched as the skins were hauled from the water and carefully shaken. In this way much gold was collected, and it is interesting to note that this procedure gave rise to one of the legends of the Golden Fleece.

The goldsmiths of Chenhu-Daro developed the granulation process, a superb technical accomplishment inspired by the form of a mimosa flower. This is a method of decorating a metal base with tiny granules usually of gold or silver. Liquid metal was employed in tiny droplets which ran into identical spheroids and cooled with a slightly flattened base. By using a highly polished surface on which the droplets formed a design, a noticeable effect of raised and hollow areas was created.

As did the tribes and races before them, the Sumerians, the Greeks, and the Etruscans loved gold, not only for its beauty but also because they found that they could create easily with it. Conscious of the play of light and shadow as an effective element in design, they employed the granulation process to great advantage in small areas of decoration. Designs of flowers, leaves, buds, and vines were thus carried out, and they copied the pomegranate and lotus, as well as other forms from nature, with great skill.

The Sumerians and Etruscans learned to carve gems and employed all kinds of plant materials as models. Early tools of flint and stone were given plant names suggestive of their shape, such as laurel-leaf point and willow-leaf knife. The Greeks in turn learned these processes from the Etruscans and were able to produce a gold thread called "fairy gold," as fine as an eyelash. Its beautiful color was likened to the "sweetness of slow-dropping honey." Gold models of the European acorn decorated many necklaces and charms, and a certain type of jewelry called "bullae" was much used. This was a hollow, convex amulet case which the Etruscans filled with nard, an aromatic resin giving off a pleasant odor when warmed by the heat of the body—the Chanel No. 5 of 4000 B.C.!

Gem carvings showing flowers of Biblical days give us clear historical proof. The anemone (the Biblical lily of the field), narcissus, daisy, and buttercup were copied. In Persia as far back as 2400 B.C. there are records of the melon carved in stone. These were of the cantaloupe variety, although Pliny, writing of them in the 1st century, described them as a variety of cucumber. The generic origin of the honeydew melon is lost in antiquity, but its striking form carved out of amber, sardonyx, lapis, and even obsidian was used extensively in necklaces and bracelets.

Throughout the centuries flowers and plants have been influential in design. The mosaic is a case in point. During the early centuries after the birth of Christ, mosaics were the primary means for depicting floral motifs. During the 10th, 11th, and 12th centuries, however, flower designs in jewelry were again developed to a great degree, but by then the fashion in dress influenced the type of jewelry worn.

During these years, for instance, clothing with high collars, frilly and lacy ruffles or embroidered silks made the wearing of stone and metal necklaces impractical. However, pearl necklaces were worn because these were smooth and not apt to damage delicate fabrics.

After the 12th century, necklaces of all kinds were again in favor. But not until the 15th century were stones faceted with any degree of scientific planning. Diamonds, emeralds, rubies, and sapphires now were cut to increase and intensify their inherent beauty.

An interesting relationship between plants and gems lies in the unit of measure for weighing precious stones. Long ago it was discovered that the seed of the carob or Quirrat tree (a type of locust tree growing in India and in Mediterranean countries) remained constant in weight no matter how dried or old it became. This seed, of the variety known as *Ceretonia siliqua,* maintained the weight of 3.20 grains troy; hence it was established as the standard of weight for all precious stones. So today we have the unit of weight called "carat" (from Quirrat).

During the Victorian era, much lavish carving went into jewelry. Flowers were superimposed on flowers; vines and leaves on stems were carved in gold, silver, copper, and the less expensive pinchbeck gold, which was not really gold at all but a heavy composition of alloys made to look like gold.

To the present day, jewelry designers find that gold, platinum, and other precious metals—with or without gems—have the greatest sale value if themes from nature form the basis of the pattern. Advertisements reveal a preference for floral forms in jewelry of precious and semiprecious stones. Such jewelry has universal appeal; it will never go out of fashion, nor will it ever become obsolete.

1. *PRECIOUS STONES*

✦ DIAMOND ✦

Though the same sun with all-diffusive rays
Blush in the rose, and in the diamond blaze
We prize the effort of His stronger power,
And justly set the gem above the flower.
—Louis Dieulafait

For flower-lovers there lies within this verse reason to do some proselytizing in the cause of horticulture. Of course, to do so would require a re-education of the poet's powers of perception, and since the quotation is from another century, the change is extremely unlikely!

But let us read the words again. Even though we may not subscribe completely to the thought encompassed, we cannot deny a parallel of appreciation. Both flowers and gems have beauty in themselves, complete and satisfying—but how that beauty is increased and enhanced when gem and flower exist in combination!

In the rough state the diamond appears to be nothing but a lump of crystal. It is so unattractive that it is hard to realize that when the stone is cut and polished the diamond is one of the most desirable of stones; it embodies intense beauty of color and durability and remains unchanged throughout the centuries.

The name, diamond, comes from the Greek word *adamas,* meaning indomitable. Excessively hard as the diamond is, the name is quite appropriate, since the stone maintains its place above all else as the hardest substance known to man.

The diamond was first mined in India, taken from the Golconda Mines. The mines produced so many diamonds that the name remains the synonym for great wealth. These mines are no longer worked, for they have been exhausted, but other mines in South America and South Africa are in constant operation. Although this stone is found in quantity in but few locations, its beauty has been carried to every corner of the world.

The diamond has a remarkable ability to refract and reflect light rays. The light from the sun is composed of all the colors of the spectrum. We see the rainbow as a band of color because a ray of light in passing through a moisture particle (a tiny prism) has been broken into its component parts, and we see those hues which are visible to the human eye: red, orange, yellow, green, blue, and violet. Scientists refer to this process as "refraction, reflection, and dispersion of the colors of the spectrum." The same thing takes place when white light hits the cut surface of a diamond. The many facets of the diamond produce a multiplicity of moving shafts of refracted light, reflected and seen by the eye as the sparkle, the fire—in short, the flash of the diamond.

Many are the stories, both true and legendary, about the diamond. Tales of mystery and intrigue, of romance and tragedy have followed the famous diamonds of the world. Volumes could be written about this one stone alone, as indeed there have been.

One such story from the book *Minerals, Metals and Gems* by A. Hyatt Verrill tells of an interesting incident which took place while the author was in British Guiana. Two diamond miners, looking for stones in the alluvial deposits along a river bed, came upon a large red crystal. One insisted it was a red diamond, but the other insisted they must test it to be sure. Finally, they agreed to strike the stone with a heavy object, reasoning that if it were a diamond it would be indestructible. What they failed to realize was that although the diamond is the hardest substance, it is brittle and can be shattered by such a blow.

The diamond shattered. But the beauty of the fragments was so appealing that they kept a few. In Georgetown they showed their "pretty treasure" to a jeweler. To their dismay they had shattered not only a rare, but probably priceless, red diamond of at least 30 carats!

It has been recorded that in Italy in the 16th century the great jeweler-artist, Cellini, was for many months a political prisoner. He grew distraught and in his melancholy state of mind was sure his enemies were trying to kill him. In his food one day he saw the glint of something sparkling. He imagined it was diamond dust carefully hidden in his food to assure his death. For hours he tortured himself with thoughts of dying. Finally he thought to test the hardness of the glinting slivers. To his relief he was able with a knife to crush the splinters against the stone wall. The story goes that his enemies actually did plot to kill him by this means, but that Cellini owed his life to the greedy jailer to whom the task was entrusted. The jailer, thinking the diamond much too valuable to be thus wasted, kept it for himself and used citrine particles in its place. Apparently the size of the fragments was not large enough to injure Cellini; his ruggedness as an individual defeated the attempt to do away with him.

Some of the most interesting tales are those connected with famous stones in national treasuries. One of the most musical names, I think, is "Kohinoor," a very famous stone now among the Crown Jewels of England. The name, Kohinoor, means "mountain of light." This diamond was found in India 5,000 years ago and was kept in Delhi until the Persian invasion, when it was taken away by what seems to have been a tragic event. It was the custom in those ancient days for the conqueror and the conquered to exchange turbans as a gesture of peace. The dethroned emperor suffered a double loss, for his beautiful "Kohinoor" was hidden in the folds of his turban, and he had to see his priceless treasure given to his enemy.

Perhaps one of the most famous stones is the Hope diamond. Its color is a magnificent deep blue, fully as deep as the color of the finest sapphire, but it has a colder, deeper luster and much more brilliance. In size it is the largest blue diamond yet discovered— 44 carats. It is square cut and of magnificent proportions. The story begins again in India, where it is said to have been found in the eye of an idol as a stone three times its present weight. A French traveler named Tavernier brought it to France and wrote of it in the account of his travels. After being lost to historians for a long time, the diamond turned up in England. Thomas Hope, for whom the stone is now named, brought it to the United States, where it was eventually sold to the McLean family of Washington, D.C.

Many years ago I met a one-time owner of the Hope diamond. I was visiting some friends in New Hampshire, and we were out for a ride in the country. My hostess stopped at a small cottage tucked away on a little side road, and here a former owner of the Hope diamond lived. True to the many legends built up around this stone, it had brought her misfortune and unhappiness.

Later it was acquired by the famous New York jeweler, Harry Winston, who in turn gave it to the government of the United States to add to the collection of gems and precious stones. Today it is on display at the Smithsonian Institution in Washington, D.C.

2. DIAMOND. A large blue-white, round cut diamond of excellent quality shows the many colors found in this precious stone. (Courtesy of N. W. Ayer & Son, New York.)

3. DIAMOND COMPOSITION. An effect of sparkle is achieved by the selection of a many-faceted glass container and the fanlike placement of background leaves. Emanating from within the body of the design, yellow roses, pink sweet peas, blue Chinese bellflowers, lavender alium, and white gypsophila provide a contrast of colors. Calla lilies and white roses lend richness of texture.

4. COLORED DIAMONDS IN THE ROUGH. These stones illustrate the many colors of diamonds. (Courtesy of De Beers Consolidated Mines, Ltd.)

▷ 5. AFRICAN DIAMOND COMPOSITION. Since it is difficult to depict in flowers the fabulous glitter and sparkle of diamonds, the locale of Africa, in which diamonds are found, is the basis for this design. A carved negroid head is elevated on a large wooden base. In back are long tropical leaves, such as those found in Africa, and red carnations (representing the story of the red diamond) spread to both sides. Long fingerlike leaves of variegated dracaena are suggestive of hands. A large, rough crystal formation is placed at the right.

From time immemorial the emerald has been used in the crowns of kings and queens, and in other royal accouterments. With a brilliant green of pure hue and intensity, the stone has great appeal.

The purest and deepest color is best brought out by faceting. This allows the stone to display more sparkle and flash. If the emerald is of a slightly milky or cloudy appearance it is cut *en cabochon,* that is, rounded and polished. However, another style of cut sometimes employed is called "emerald cut," which means cut with a flat, rectangular top and with facets around the edges. This style is cut fairly deeply which, of course, adds to the stone's depth of color and intensity of brilliance. The term "emerald cut" is not confined to emeralds alone but is often used in describing diamonds, or any other stone cut in this style.

In ancient times many emeralds were cut in the round form. They did not always have as many facets as they do today. A cloudy stone shows more beautifully when cut *en cabochon.* To some people the silky inclusions in the stone increase its beauty; this, however, is a matter of personal taste.

It also becomes a matter of cost: the purest and most intense green is the finest stone, therefore the most expensive. Like all other precious stones, the value must be determined by the beauty— the sheer beauty and appeal of the stone. For instance if a stone of one carat costs $500, a stone of four carats would not necessarily cost four times as much; instead it could cost as much as $5,000. This increased ratio is the case with all precious stones, since nature generally produces these very beautiful gems in rather small sizes; larger stones, because of their rarity, are of much greater value.

The emerald is of the beryl family and is found in many places, in India and South America in particular. The early Egyptians mined emeralds, but it is believed that after a few centuries their mines ran out and that subsequently they obtained their emeralds from the Far East.

When interpreting the emerald, since green in its purest hue and full intensity is the color of the finest emeralds, flower arrangers are

▷ 6. EMERALD COMPOSITION. The elegance of the emerald suggested the use of a formal, severely simple style; thus a clear crystal container with green bowl inset is used here. Clivia and Hawaiian ginger leaves were selected for their pure green, while the cypripedium orchids represent the lighter green values sometimes found in emeralds. A tiny teakwood stand displays two emeralds of a milky cast. The rough, uncut stones on the base contain emerald crystals. A pin containing a marquise emerald and a pearl bracelet with square-cut emerald clasp complete the design.

interested in the brightest green in plant material. Although emerald color has been described as grass green, this is not accurate. Allowing for differences in textural surfaces, the leaf of the nasturtium or of the episcea is much closer to the purity of emerald green and quite satisfactory for interpretation. Shiny and reflective green leaves, such as those of the southern magnolia or the lustrous sheen of a clustered rosette of *Pieris japonica*, could also be used.

Bells of Ireland have a fresh, vivid, but lighter value of green, and because they have centers containing small white dots suggesting the reflective sparkle of the emerald, they too are a good choice for interpretation. Jack-in-the-pulpit has a light tint of green and is perhaps the nearest to transparency that may be found in the plant world.

Pale emeralds with silky inclusions are nearly opaque. The silver-leaf, or *leucodendron,* covered with a fine, hairlike growth, is comparable in appearance to the stone and so can be used in interpretation.

It is very easy to duplicate the true color of emeralds in glass; therefore, the use of a green glass container is appropriate in interpretation. Water will intensify the sparkle if chunks of glass are placed inside the container. A monochromatic effect is easily achieved with green leaves, but a few green Fuji chrysanthemums will enhance the design through contrast of color value and texture.

When attempting to interpret any stone which has transparency and sparkle, it is wise to do some research, for from it an idea, possibly by association, is bound to evolve. For example, in my research I came upon an interesting story which could be the inspiration for an arrangement. An old tree, blown over in a very high wind, left roots exposed. Among the roots were many small green stones glittering in the sunshine—emeralds! We never know what lies deeply hidden under our very feet; we never know when some unexpected find will come to light by mere chance. Serendipity! Our earth must hold many unknown surprises to delight and enchant us!

It would seem that a mound of moss—fine, closely knit, and of deep green intensity—is a good example of emerald green. Because of the fine, threadlike stems, the textural quality of the moss is concentrated and takes on a deep velvety appearance. Many of nature's green leaves contain blue or yellow in their color. Fern fronds and ivy leaves, selected for a minimum content of yellow and blue, could also be used. Although opaque in essence, the silky sheen of the green-and-white tulip is a pleasant parallel which could be used to advantage.

44

✦ RUBY ✦

> *This stone has the coloring of a freshly opened rose.*
> *The light shines right through it and yet is reflected by*
> *it at the same time, emerging ruby-colored, purified, as*
> *by a fire which leaves no ashes. It's alive! It breathes*
> *in sunshine or lamplight. It 'lives!'*
>
> —JOSEPH KESSEL

How true this statement is. The finest rubies, alive with fire and beauty, are called pigeon blood, and this properly describes the hue, for these rubies are of a rich, velvety, wonderfully deep red. The finest are cut *en cabochon,* which allows the concentration of color to be diffused gently but with intensity. Some rubies, of course, are faceted so that the light striking the stone is reflected with flash and sparkle. When the color of a ruby is of gem quality, it matches the center of the red band on the color spectrum: a pure red hue of full intensity.

Lighter colored rubies are faceted, since this increases their sparkle and effectiveness. One type of semiprecious stone, called spinel, is a poppy red and was believed for centuries to be a ruby, the color being nearly identical. Another is the balas, which is a slightly bluish red. Neither is difficult to interpret in flower arrangements, since intense sparkle is not one of their characteristics. Red poppies, slightly tinged with orange, are excellent for depicting the delicate, fragile color of the spinel "ruby." The foliage of poppy is good too, since it adds fine lines which are like inclusions in a ruby. The balas "ruby" may be well interpreted with beebalm *(Monarda),* for its hue is tinged with blue.

Paler in color than a pigeon blood, but especially beautiful, is the star ruby, an example of a phenomenon known as asterism. This gem, regardless of the way it is turned, shows a six-point star across the top of its domed cabochon shape, formed by microscopic shafts of light within the body of the stone which intersect at the apex and channel the light rays into soft, whitish straight lines. Although normally the star ruby is no larger than 20 carats, there is a larger one in existence which belonged to the Fourth Earl of Ashburnham (1797–1878), which is said to be 500 million years old. Found in Ceylon, this particular star ruby is 138 carats in weight. Surprisingly, its color is a shocking pink!

The star ruby may be interpreted in a flower arrangement by using pink roses of medium color value; their texture is exactly right for the smooth, satiny glow of this stone. Combined with it and subtly placed, artemisia with its grayish green foliage suggests the rays of the star.

Because of their hardness—next to that of the diamond, in fact— the durability of rubies is unquestioned. Rarely are they carved, although a few have inscription on them. In the Odescalchi Museum in Italy, for example, according to an account in *Precious Stones* published in 1874, there is a ruby engraved with a design representing Ceres holding an ear of corn.

The ruby has been the jewel of kings for as long as there have been kingdoms. Before kings could write, scribes were hired to prepare official edicts, and the king would put his seal, cut in stone, to the parchment. Although ruby would have been the logical choice, it was not possible to use it because it adhered too tightly to wax. Therefore the seals were cut from carnelian, a stone readily found and carved.

The finest rubies have for centuries come from Mogok, the "valley of rubies" in Burma. Still mined by the most primitive methods, there are many stones taken from the mine which are not of gem quality. Some are too dark and dull; others are too light and pale. All are taken to the owner-operator of the mine and classified, even before polishing or faceting. Then, except for those which show promise of pigeon-blood quality, they are displayed for sale in the market place.

Travelers say they have seen many open market places, but none so colorful as the one in Tchaipin in Upper Burma. This market place is described as surrounded by mystery and suspense, with an

▷ 7. RUBY AND SAPPHIRE COMPOSITION. This display depicts the products of the market place in Mogok, Burma. A large brass Moradabad tray, incised with a design in red and green, displays the chosen items. In the actual markets, uncut stones are often placed on a foundation of leaves, so here red-striped dracaena is used. Delicate temple bells, cinnamon sticks, fruits and tomatoes, with rows of uncut rubies and sapphires arranged on each side of the tray, represent the offerings of the market. The tiny, bright red straw flowers, green laurel, and maidenhair fern are arranged in the casual manner typical of Mogok. (Another possibility, and just as characteristic, would be to lay on the tray large colorful leaves of dracaena, ti or croton, folded, braided, or knotted into designs displaying the gems on these foliage patterns.)

atmosphere of excitement penetrating it all. Most of the people thronging the narrow road are Oriental, with a few English, French, and Americans joining them. All are intent on pursuing the magnificent pigeon-blood ruby and its sister gem, the sapphire.

At the market place rows of fruit, herbs, vegetables, silks, and linens are displayed with the inevitable rubies and sapphires. Sometimes the stones are displayed alone, but most striking and colorful are the large displays on brass or copper trays with goods, such as tomatoes, berries, small temple bells, flowers, etc., arranged on the edges and down through the center, framed with rows of rubies and sapphires.

There are, of course, other stones of beauty in the family of red stones. One is the almandine, a stone of a soft lavender-red, known for centuries. Garnet, too, is a very old stone; the *Bible* mentions it as one of the stones in the breastplate of Aaron. Garnets are found in many localities, but they are so common in Asia that during the war in Kashmir (1892), when the Hanza tribes fought the British, they were used as bullets. And according to legend, garnets were so brilliant they were used to light Noah's Ark.

▷ 8. RUBY AND SAPPHIRE COMPOSITION. Because the ruby and sapphire are "sisters under the skin," these two colors are combined here in an Indian mosaic theme. A frame through which the flowers were inserted is used to create this patterned effect. The intense red of Happiness roses matches the pigeon-blood rubies at the lower left. The cornflower, which in Burma is the color associated with sapphire, perfectly interprets this stone. Deep blue delphinium adds variety, and a touch of baby's breath gives the effect of sparkle. The delicate green of the springerai not only represents another color found in sapphires but suggests the richness of the Mogok locale.

9. RUBY. This beautiful Burmese ruby is a pendant carved *en cabochon* in the form of a rooster. (Courtesy of the American Museum of Natural History, New York.)

▷ 10. RUBY AND LASER LIGHT. This truly modern interpretation of laser light suggests its link with the ruby. Intense red roses and a modern decorative product, "plastic rain," are used in conjunction with curved strips of translucent plastic fastened to a transparent plastic base. Laser is the acronym meaning "Light Amplification by Stimulated Emission of Radiation." The development of laser light came through the persistent efforts of a scientist who made use of a ruby in his experiments. The light is generated and passed through the stone, after which it races toward its object. Laser light rays are the most powerful light beams yet developed. They are of extremely narrow radius and have a degree of directional accuracy so powerful that if focused by means of a lens they can burn holes in a diamond or vaporize any material known.

Long ago, many Chinese became wealthy merchants by buying and selling sapphires. Because they have universal appeal, sapphires have found their way all over the world. Like rubies they are mined in Mogok, but sapphires are also found in quantity in Ceylon. Dating back to a very remote period, the mining of sapphires has been an important industry there.

Although sapphires are composed of corundum, the same basic mineral as rubies, the inclusion of other minerals in minute quantities gives sapphires varying degrees of color. The finest and rarest are of a deep, rich, velvety blue which matches the hue of the cornflower. In fact from earliest times, "cornflower blue" has been used to describe the finest quality sapphires.

Star sapphires are well known, but like the ruby they are of a paler hue than the stone of gem quality. A soft sky-blue is their usual color, rather grayish and misty. While the texture of a rose is perfect for interpreting the star ruby, it is unsuitable for the star sapphire; the best effect is achieved by using a blue forget-me-not, or a flower of similar color when interpreting sapphires. Florets of the blue hydrangea, if clustered carefully, are another possibility. In a large arrangement, light blue iris would be a good choice, or the palest blue delphinium. Both have a lustrous character to supply the tonal qualities needed in an interpretation of this stone.

Black star sapphires have rarely been found, but there is one of note which is a rich, dark gray. This is a very large stone of 2,095 carats. The famous stone is a reverse intaglio carved by Harry Dorian in the likeness of Dwight D. Eisenhower. The only reverse intaglio cabochon in history, this magnificent piece is on display at the Smithsonian Institution, Washington, D.C. If you are fortunate enough to see this famed gray sapphire, note the fascinating play of light on its surface. Although texturally the stone is hard and shiny, it lacks sparkle, so that light shining on the stone is muted, in opposition to the expected brilliance of a hard surface. The reason for this unusual property is that its deep shading absorbs so much light that the asterism is the only reflective quality left.

Sapphires are found in other colors: yellow, green, lavender, pink, and even white. If as a flower arranger you interpret the sapphire, you might well include all the pastel colors, plus, of course, the intense blue which typifies the beautiful sapphire.

Like rubies, sapphires are sold in the open market places in Mogok. It is interesting to note that the white sapphires displayed are always faceted in order to increase their brilliance.

If you wish to be completely original and can obtain the necessary materials, an excellent choice for interpretation would be the highly treasured orange sapphire. This rare gem is called *padparadshah* in India, its country of origin (in Sanskrit it means "the color of the lotus blossom"). The particular lotus to which this undoubtedly refers must have tints more orange than pink. The flower has a highly treasured sheen which no other flower possesses to the same degree.

2. *SEMIPRECIOUS STONES*

✦ ALEXANDRITE ✦

Alexandrite is a stone with twin personalities in that it has the remarkable quality of pleochroism. This means that the structural makeup of the stone is such that when natural light strikes its surface, the light is reflected back, showing only a bottle-green color. When the stone is taken into artificial light, however, it appears to be raspberry red. The stone is shiny and rather vitreous in appearance but lacks the brilliance associated with the emerald or ruby, even when it is cut with facets. In other words, alexandrite appears as a solid: not opaque, but also not transparent.

Found in the Ural Mountains in Russia on the day in 1833 when Czar Alexander II came of age, the stone was named for the young Czar. It has since been found elsewhere, but the finest quality alexandrite comes from the original place in Russia. To distinguish this unusual Russian stone which shows definite qualities of red and green, it is referred to as "gem-quality alexandrite." This does not mean that it is classified in jeweler's terminology as a gem or precious stone. It simply means that there is a distinction between this stone, which shows definite red and green, and other stones which have an alexandritelike quality but which more commonly show paler lavender to light green tints.

There are some very beautiful alexandrite stones. A large size of about ten carats in an "emerald cut" may cost as much as $10,000. This size has great eye-appeal and fascination for the collector. Something very mysterious seems lurking in its depths: one wonders why, by merely changing the quality of light rays, this stone changes color. A fascinating and rare stone it is.

▷ 11. ALEXANDRITE ARRANGEMENT. Roses are used here to depict the red aspect of alexandrite and philodendron leaves to represent its green quality. The tall alium is placed in this design for its interesting curves as well as to suggest the lavender color frequently found in stones of pleochromatic nature.

12. AMAZONITE. This stone is basically light green with occasional areas of a deeper rich green.

✦ AMAZONITE ✦

In many respects amazonite is similar to aventurine, another semi-precious stone. However, amazonite contains more white in its makeup and reveals clearly marked splotches and streaks of bright green, looking somewhat like dye spots.

For interpretation, a selection of plant material with green and white in its coloration is easy to find. Funkia leaves, green chrysanthemums, and bells of Ireland are all possibilities. Caladium leaves with a large amount of white are a good choice. One of the most interesting possible materials is the donya, a bush which grows in the southern hemisphere. It has small, ovate green leaves with one white leaf at the end of each branch. This single leaf flutters almost constantly, giving a varying effect of green and white ideal for interpretation of this stone. As a suggestion, this leaf would combine very effectively with lily of the valley.

Keep in mind that opaque stones such as amazonite (and aventurine) should not be interpreted using plant material with a shiny and translucent texture, for example, the leaves of magnolia, laurel, or gardenia. Because these stones are opaque and matte in texture, their appearance is less refined and elegant than that of sparkling gems. Flowers such as hydrangea with its many small florets, or any of the clustered flowers for that matter, are better suited. Texturally comparison is important. Light rays striking the surface of these stones are controlled by the broken texture of their makeup; they are not coarse stones, but neither are they as elegant or refined as the precious stones.

13. AMAZONITE ARRANGEMENT. This simple yet expressive design is variation No. 2 of the Upright Style as taught in the Sogetsu School of Ikebana. Branches with small leaves and greenish white lilies present a true likeness to amazonite.

56

There is a wonderful story of how amethyst was given its name. According to Greek mythology, Bacchus was greatly incensed and angry over an imagined slight by the Goddess Diana. As he wandered through a forest brooding over his hurt, he threatened to set his pack of wild dogs upon the first creature he met. As it happened, he came upon a beautiful young maiden on her way to worship at Diana's shrine. Bacchus immediately ordered his wild beasts to tear her to pieces. Diana, hearing the young maiden's cries for help, quickly turned her into a pure white stone. Bacchus, seeing the dreadful fate which had befallen the girl, became very contrite. To redeem himself he poured a large quantity of his precious wine over the stone, and before his eyes it became amethyst. To this day true amethyst is the color of deep purple wine.

Legends coming to us from Greek mythology say that anyone wearing an amethyst is immune to intoxication and will never fall under the influence of wines. We wonder if Bacchus was aware of this belief because if so, his faith was certainly misplaced. Since he was the god of wine and revelry, with his love of feasts and the accompanying wines which flowed so freely, artists usually depicted him bedecked with grapes and amethysts.

For centuries these lovely stones have been used in necklaces and rings, and it is the amethyst that graces the hands of bishops and prelates.

Many amethysts are pale but sparkling. Others are of deeper value and must be "looked into" and studied in order to absorb their magnificent depth of color. The finest amethysts are, of course, deeply colored. When clear, they are faceted in many styles. But, if the stones are clouded or, like emeralds, have silky inclusions, they are more beautiful when cut *en cabochon*. Amethysts of the quartz family are fairly common and are not difficult to carve.

▷ 14. AMETHYST COMPOSITION. Pale lavender delphinium appears at the top. Purple larkspur stand behind for depth and also are arranged on the left side. The purple delphinium was selected because it has a layer of light blue petals, so lovely with purple anemones. One anemone has a reddish cast, while the other introduces the violet color of the stone; they also provide contrast of form. For color variation, and because rose quartz is so often used with amethyst, pink Sensation roses are included. Delphinium foliage, selected for its beautiful curve, is arranged to follow the flow and swirl of the figurine's robe. A cluster of amethyst crystals in the rough and a 63-carat amethyst in its faceted and polished beauty on the purple mat complete the composition.

Even so, remember that there are degrees of beauty and quality set by the intensity and clarity of the stone's hue.

An amethyst has its own delightful way of beckoning to the observer. To me, the stone has several personalities. It may have a reddish cast (still within the purple body of the stone), or it may have a bluish cast, making the stone appear blue-violet. The deep intensity of Parma violets is a perfect likeness or parallel to the blue-violet amethyst.

I have long looked for glassware of the true amethyst color, but seldom have I been able to find the intense blue-violet coloring. Very often, so-called amethyst glass is a reddish purple, and not especially satisfying to the eye.

As for plant material, compatible textural qualities are found in the purple delphinium. Note the blue petals (making the flower bi-colored), which often grow as part of this flower. The eye tends to mix the two hues, and the effect of blue-violet is the result. The tiny white centers in the purple delphinium give the effect of the subdued sparkle of a faceted amethyst.

Purple gloxinia is a fine choice for an accent flower—and keep in mind Parma violets; a cluster of them is delightful. Both are deep, velvety, and wonderfully rich textured in feeling; both depict the amethyst color beautifully. Clematis (the Jackmani variety), a deep blue-purple in color, is a satisfactory likeness, and so too are purple larkspur or purple and violet anemones.

✦ AQUAMARINE ✦

Aquamarine, like the emerald, is a member of the beryl family of minerals. This stone is found in great quantities in South America; some very large ones are exhibited by jewelers from time to time. Aquamarine is a transparent stone and therefore is generally faceted or cut in the style known as emerald cut. In color, the stone is described as a deep bluish green; it varies in degrees of blue. Since the mother color is light blue-green, its name, aquamarine, is very appropriate, the touch of watery blue giving the stone a clear, delightfully cool appearance. Very small aquamarines are nearly always pale in color. A larger size stone, because of its volume, is a deeper blue-green.

Texturally the aquamarine is hard, cold and shiny, rather vitreous in effect. Because of its brilliance, sparkle, and purity of hue, it is the most difficult of transparent stones to interpret in flower arrangements. In fact, it is the only stone which presents so great a challenge to the arranger. It required research to discover a proper background or historical fact as a point of beginning. I found my cue in learning that the aquamarine was the only stone faceted by the early Romans and that they held it in high esteem. Wherever emeralds are found, there too aquamarines are to be found. Since the ancient Egyptians had emerald mines, probably much of the aquamarine used in Rome came from the mines of Egypt.

▷ 15. AQUAMARINE COMPOSITION. Arranged in a formal style, this composition presents a tribute to Rome, where formality and elegance characterized the days of empire. Plaster and clay replicas of Corinthian columns, made by an Italian artist, set this mood. Because of the lack of fresh flowers appropriate to an interpretation of the aquamarine, feathery field flowers—goldenrod, wild aster, Queen Anne's lace, and papyrus from the lily pond—were used before they dried, and all were sprayed with light blue-green paint. Before the paint dried, glitter dust was scattered over the flowers. Enough adhered to give the subtle sparkle desired, thus recreating the exact effect of the stone in an objective arrangement.

Aventurine, a light green stone, is composed of minerals in which very minute crystals are arranged in random fashion, producing an effect of a great number of silvery flecks in the stone. Its best interpretation, it would seem, is in the use of artemisia which has the same grayish, silvery effect.

Aventurine has been carved for centuries into the likeness of stems, leaves, flowers, and buds. During the early Egyptian era, when the lavish use of semiprecious stones was the order of the day, aventurine was carved into the shapes of poppy buds and seed pods, acorns, laurel leaves, and pomegranates. Influenced by lands to the east as trading increased, the Egyptians used aventurine to carve an especially attractive form, the cardamon seed, like a round melon with deeply incised segments. An image of the scarab, a beetle sacred to the ancient Egyptians, cut from this semiprecious stone was much favored and frequently worn as a charm or amulet. This form has continued in usage throughout the centuries, and even today paperweights, jewelry, trinket boxes, and jar covers are carved with the scarab motif.

Aventurine is found in many places throughout the world, especially in India, where it is still mined in great quantity. It has appeared on the markets throughout the Far East and has, unfortunately, been called "Indian Jade" by many dealers. Since it is not jade, and in color only vaguely resembles jade, it is being sold under an incorrect name. In some cases this stone is dyed to intensify its green color, but this is at the expense of the true silvery fleck, so interesting and characteristic of aventurine.

According to an article in a Japanese daily paper, Communist China is engaged in producing carved "jade" figurines in great quantity. There is a huge demand for this art, and no doubt the sale of green figurines, no matter what the composition, would be increased if the magic name of jade were used in connection with green stone.

▷ 16. AVENTURINE COMPOSITION. This is a study of similarities in color and texture. The figure of the goddess in long flowing robe, who holds a lotus flower and leaves in her right hand, inspired the elongated design. Tall aspidistra leaves, twisted on each side for effects of shadow and light, accent the uplifted line of the carving. Because some aventurine has a grayish green cast, long-stemmed, ribbed funkia leaves of similar color are used. Two small, naturally curled water-lily leaves are placed at the lower left, and half-opened water lilies appear on the lower right side of the composition. (Lotus flowers and leaves would do as well.)

17. BLOODSTONE. Three of these pieces of bloodstone have edges rounded by tumbling and polishing; the fourth was carved on a lapidary wheel into a heart shape. They all show a deep rich green with small red spots like drops of blood.

▷ 18. BLOODSTONE ARRANGEMENT. Cineraria blossoms with the red coloring of the bloodstone and begonia leaves with the iron-cross pattern were selected for this simple yet dignified design. Palm, associated with the Holy Land, is used here to suggest the arms of the cross.

✦ BLOODSTONE ✦

An especially interesting stone is the bloodstone—dark green with blood-red spots running through it. Many superstitions and legends are attached to the bloodstone, some dating from the Crucifixion of Christ. This semiprecious stone can be called "the dogwood of the mineral world," for as one legend tells us the bloodstone, like this little woodland tree, played a part in the Crucifixion. According to legend, the blood of Christ dropped on the stone which lay at the foot of the cross, and forever after this stone was marked by red spots. The cross itself, legend has it, was fashioned from the dogwood tree. The white bracts enclosing the flower clusters on the tree carry pinched, discolored tips put there, so legend goes, by the cruel nails which impaled Christ to the wood.

Through the years the bloodstone has been beautifully carved by artists utilizing the red spots to function importantly in the design; sometimes they have shown up as beads around the throat of a model, or as other ornamentation worn by carved figures. Carvings of the head of Christ have even utilized the red spots so that droplets of blood seem to fall from the torturous crown of thorns.

The bloodstone seems to hold great appeal for men. Because of its dark and weighty appearance, the stone is especially appropriate for men's jewelry; it is particularly effective when set in a heavy gold ring.

With its smooth and glossy texture and very dark color, the bloodstone has only surface reflection. These qualities, plus its opaqueness, make the stone easy to interpret in a flower arrangement; it has many parallel likenesses in plant material. An excellent choice would be croton leaves, especially those with red splotches and streaks. Combined with red carnations or anemones, symbolic of the fields of lilies of Biblical days, a good interpretation could be achieved.

<h1 style="text-align:center">✦ CRYSTAL ✦</h1>

Rock crystal, a colorless transparent quartz, is one of the commonest minerals. The most desirable crystal is perfectly clear, like "frozen water," the Chinese say, because it is cold to the touch. The unmistakable appearance of the clear rock is due to its texture, which is unmarked by any particular strata, lines, or inclusions. It is its unique texture, however, which sets crystal apart from glass; its transparent, icy luster marks it as a jeweler's stone. But even possessing these qualities, crystal still lacks the fire and sparkle of the diamond.

The familiar rhinestone is a clear crystal quartz. The name "rhinestone" is aptly applied, since the stone is found in the Rhine River. It comes, however, from many other parts of the world as well. There are many sources of crystal which offer pieces large enough to be fashioned into sizable objects. Since the days of the earliest civilizations, artists have carved crystal, and the practice continues today.

"Fondling pieces" were extremely popular during the luxurious and extravagant days of the courts of French kings. Ladies of the aristocracy held crystal forms in their hands to keep themselves cool as they rode in their carriages on hot, humid days.

In the old embroidery centers of French Indo-China, the girls working on white linen and fine cloth were supplied with crystal forms or pebbles. They were expected to hold them from time to time to cool their hands, thus preventing perspiration from staining the fine linens and laces.

Fondling pieces have been made from other substances too—jade, agate, and sardonyx—all of them cold to the touch. Thus the habit of holding small, smooth pieces of stone and running one's fingers over them, or playing with them in the hand, has been a kind of tranquilizer. As tension relievers, certainly they are less harmful than today's sleeping pill or the proffered cigarette!

In an antique shop one day, I found a veritable prize of square-cut crystals set in silver and exhibiting beautiful workmanship—the clearest, coldest, and most limpid stones I had ever seen in crystal. They were called "Chanel crystal," the shopkeeper explained. Can you recall the early years of this century when "Chanel crystals" enjoyed popularity? Usually they were cut in a round, "brilliant" (to borrow from the diamond) form and set in a black chain, looped several times around the neck. Sometimes a watch was fastened to the chain and carefully tucked into the wide sash worn around the waist. I remember well my mother wearing one and very carefully adjusting the silk sash to completely cover and hold the watch safely.

Genuine crystal, when smoothly polished, glows with a soft, diffused light; it does not sparkle or flash, but has a soft, glowing, limpid quality. When it is faceted it shows only mild sparkle.

▷ 19. CRYSTAL COMPOSITION. A tall English toasting glass suggests the elegance of this stone and sets the tone of the design. White flowers predominate, but the few pastel-colored blossoms are in keeping with the fragile appearance of the glass and add a pleasing variety. The delicately petaled flowers, such as petunia, daisy, Queen Anne's lace, and pale pink geranium used here, give an excellent interpretation of this stone's reflective quality. A small polished crystal elephant and the two chunks of uncut crystal complete the design. (This arrangement could be considered suitable for a diamond interpretation as well, since the clarity of crystal is similar to that of the diamond.)

Richard Gump calls jade the "Stone of Heaven." It has its beginnings in history so far back as to be almost unrecorded. From the earliest days of China, jade was used, loved, and invested with religious significance.

The term, jade, is used to designate the stone, but actually there are three separate minerals in this classification. The first and by far the oldest known group is nephrite, which has many colors in its makeup but is so classified because it contains silicate of magnesium. Chemically speaking jadeite, the second, contains a silicate of aluminum. The third group, called chloromelanite, is black or very nearly black in appearance and is of the same composition as nephrite but contains minerals which increase its dark color.

Many descriptive names have been assigned to jade; for instance, imperial jade does not indicate a particular color, although it is a beautiful apple green, but rather a quality and beauty worthy of the emperor's collection. We find in some cases that this type was reserved exclusively for royal possession; no other person, under penalty of a terrible fate, was allowed to own any jade of this special quality.

Another beautiful variation is the kingfisher jade, the name being given because it is likened to the green in the feathers of this bird. Chicken-bone jade is exactly the color of white chicken bones, and mutton-fat jade is reddish with white streaks. Could any name be more descriptive than spinach-green jade?

Beeswax jade is yellowish, having a waxy and smooth texture. Lavender jade is likened to "lavender clouds caught in drifts of green," and some of the green jade is referred to as "moss entangled in melting snow." Picturesque and descriptive, is it not? Orange-colored jade always seems to have a slight pinkish overtone—a delightful stone to study and enjoy. There are other descriptive names, some not as pleasant or musical but still semantic.

The beauty of good jade is best felt not by the senses alone, but by experiencing the delight it can evoke within one's self. When feeling the essential spirit of the stone actually takes place, it is more spiritual than the mere looking at or holding of a piece of jade. Getting the "feel" of jade means experiencing a mysterious pull on our emotions so strong that it seems to be a part of our very being.

Jade should be carved as soon after mining as possible because, like the emerald, it hardens after exposure to air. Toughness is one of jade's most important characteristics. It is hard, brittle, and fibrous in character and fractures along certain lines but does not show crystallization. It is always smooth and waxy to the touch, and heavy in the hand. It also has the unique property of giving off a melodious sound when struck as a gong. Even the writing of "jade" in Chinese is beautiful in its flowing form: 玉. Jade is *yu* in Chinese and *hisui* in Japanese.

It is interesting to note that sand and water were the first abrasives used to cut jade. Later, garnet dust was used instead of sand, and still later, corundum dust (ruby and sapphire) was used. To drill holes in jade, water and an abrasive were used with a point made of bamboo.

An amusing statement has been made about powdered jade. The ancient Chinese thought that if it were given to a sick person, it would preserve the color of his body for several years after death. Undoubtedly they neglected to consider the possibility of its hastening death! It would seem here that the means did not justify the end, but the Chinese revered their ancestors perhaps more than any other race, and to them perfect preservation meant much. A jade piece was often placed between the lips of the dead to insure their having something of value in the hereafter, and it was the driving ambition of every Chinese to own at least one piece of jade.

A Chinese of ancient days had great feeling, even reverence, for his piece of jade, and an interesting account has been given about an emperor of the Ming dynasty in China. He had a particularly fine piece of jade which he wished to have carved by the best-known artist of the day. He sent for this man and, giving him the piece of green and white nephrite, explained that he wished to have carved from it a dragon fighting two Foo dogs. Since this was a royal command, the artist could not refuse, but he could not bring himself to carve the stone as he was instructed. For several months the artist did not communicate with the emperor to report on his progress, but finally he sent a message requesting to be relieved of the commission. When summoned to the court, the artist was censured for his rashness in daring to refuse to carve as the emperor had instructed. But he explained that he simply could not see in the jade the subject which was commanded. As a Chinese he not only had an inherent and intense love for beautiful jade but the need to be true to his art. The emperor disregarded the advice of members of his court to punish the disobedient carver, and fortunately he then allowed the artist to carve what he saw in the jade. Not until two years later did the artist bring his piece of jade to the emperon. Carved in exquisite fashion, the piece of jade had become four silver carp swimming lazily through green weeds in a pool. The excess dust grindings from the carving were so small in quantity that there was scarcely enough waste left to cover the hand of the emperor. The true artist feels his subject and allows the medium to dictate the design.

Since the Chinese were more inclined than other people to love purity of form above all else, they found their highest artistic pleasure in the handling of jade fondling pieces, which also served as tension relievers and good luck pieces. The simple, smooth form was a delight to touch, and together with much religious and supernatural meaning, it lifted the soul in a kind of ecstasy which was beyond the material world of appearances.

In *A Confucian Notebook* Edward Herbert sets forth the idea that the cutting of jade into objects of art and the formation of one's character by "learning" were part of the worker's heritage. He carved ivory and sculptured jade, and as these were emblems of lengthy and laborious shaping, they also represented a refining of his moral personality.

Jade is also found in Alaska but is of quite a different appearance. It does not seem to have the same textural quality or beauty as the Khotan and Yarkand jade, but it is found in comparatively huge pieces. One piece in recent years was planned as the medium for an unusual statue, "Senora Eva Peron in Jade."

It seems that years ago in Argentina, while he was still in power, General Peron ordered a statue of his wife to be carved from Alaskan jade. A 23,000-pound block was taken from the jade mountain near Kotzebue, Alaska, but by the time it had reached the carver's knife, the political situation had changed and the order was canceled. For quite a while the block lay exposed, with tourists chipping off pieces for souvenirs. Eventually the owner had the block of jade wrapped up and stored. A 23,000-pound block of jade, even Alaskan jade, at current prices would perhaps bring $99,000, if a purchaser could be found. However, even today the Senora slumbers on in her jade prison, not yet released by the carver. Unless Argentina orders it finished, it may well become the medium for smaller statues or insignificant bits of jewelry.

Because jade may be carved so beautifully with a smooth, wax-

20. PEAR BLOSSOM AND JADE COMPOSITION. The airy feeling of space, enhanced by the strength of the dark pear-blossom branch, gives this design an atmosphere of timelessness. Natural-colored ginger root, a form frequently found in Chinese art, extends to the right in line with the carved Foo dogs atop the plinths. Small orchids with yellow-and-brown petals are placed at the right and bring a variety of color to the composition.

The jade plinths shown here are part of a three-piece set which, although not of the color or quality designated as imperial jade, is said to have been kept in the imperial treasury in Peking for the last 500 years. These very heavy pieces carved with Chinese characters are thought to date from the Han dynasty (206 B.C.–A.D. 220). (This composition was shown in a special Easter exhibition at the Montclair Art Museum, Montclair, New Jersey.)

textured result, sculptured leaves such as sanseveria, the heavy-leaved sedum, kalanchoe, chrysanthemum, and lotus are good materials for use in depicting jade carvings. Pale lavender delphinium, light pink flowers of the sedum, pale blue of the anemone, and yellow-green of early spring foliage, all may be used to interpret jade.

The leaves of the rex begonia, with their dark green sculptured surface and dark red, hairy underside, are beautiful in representing mutton-fat jade—red streaked with white. A pale yellow flower, celandine, and its own lacy, light green foliage are good for interpreting beeswax jade. Pale blue lupine has a definite affinity with blue jade.

Indian pipe, a delicate white plant devoid of chlorophyll and found in wooded areas, is an apt likeness to white Soochow jade, as is the lovely green and white caladium leaf. Artemisia, too, has the whitish quality and sculptured, serrated leaves necessary to interpret sculptured jade.

Crassula, aptly named jade plant, is often found with reddish edges; the thickness of its leaf together with its waxy, smooth surface make it very good to use. In fact, many of the sedums are acceptable.

There are at least two flowers I know of, either of which would be absolutely perfect to use in an interpretation of orange jade: the orange tuberous begonia (always with a rich glistening sheen), and the rose known as Orange Delight. I delight in using these with a jade carving to create a composition showing the warm textural likeness and the impact of exciting, compatible colors!

Please remember that some of the plant materials mentioned here are listed not only to be used in arrangement interpretation but also so you may enjoy more fully and deeply the parallel likenesses when you see these forms or their jade counterparts. Some plants, such as the Indian pipe, are not meant to be plucked for use in an interpretation but rather to be enjoyed visually in their natural state as you recall the beauty of a piece of carved white jade.

▷ 21. BEESWAX JADE COMPOSITION. The combination of plant design with the yellow-green jade figurine of a Taoist priest on the dark Oriental base produces a dramatic effect. The same foliage is used as in Plate 24: heavy sanseveria and kalanchoe leaves combine here with yellow chrysanthemums to create an Oriental mood.

◁ 22. GRAY JADEITE. This smoothly polished pendant has an unusually soft gray, cloudlike coloring. An amethyst bead acts as a holder at the top. (Courtesy of Ward's Natural Science Establishment, Rochester, New York and Monterey, California.)

▽ 23. JADE OF VARIOUS COLORS. *Top row (left to right):* One of a pair of emerald-green jade earrings, with a pearl at the earclip; yellow-gold ring (designed by the author) containing excellent examples of lavender jade set as the petals of a flower with a pearl in the center; emerald-green jade earring, companion to the one at far left. *Bottom row (left to right):* An earring of white jadeite carved as two interlocking pieces; the clasp of a necklace in orange jade with overtones of pink; a highly polished piece of brown jade; white jadeite earring, companion to the one at far left.

▷ 24. ORANGE-AND-PINK JADE ARRANGEMENT. Strong sanseveria leaves of thick texture and with light edges were chosen for this design. Smooth, heavy-petaled kalanchoe in rosette form is used at the base. In the center of the arrangement is a small wooden gate of Oriental influence, through which Orange Delight roses are arranged. These were selected for the compatibility of their rich waxy texture and satinlike sheen with jade, and because their size is in keeping with the rarity of orange-and-pink jade.

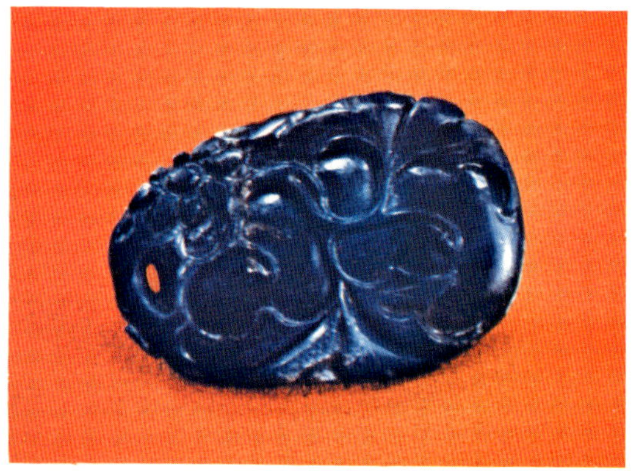

25. LAPIS LAZULI, DARK. This pendant of deeply carved lapis has a dark, rich blue color and velvety luster. (Courtesy of Ward's Natural Science Establishment, Rochester, New York and Monterey, California.)

26. LAPIS LAZULI, LIGHT. This stone cut *en cabochon* is a mottled white-and-blue lapis containing golden metallic flecks. Such pieces are often carved to utilize the blue coloring advantageously in depicting subject matter such as sky, clouds, and landscape.

▷ 27. LAPIS LAZULI ARRANGEMENT. This light and feathery design utilizes space in delightful proportion, yet is well anchored by the arresting blue containers. The two arrangements of sparsely tufted pine create a linear and spatial harmony. Clustered lobelia and blue plumbago lend color and texture to this interpretation. The tiny, clustered abelia blossoms echo the design and scale of the white flowers on the cloisonné vases, which are made of powdered lapis and a white stone.

✦ LAPIS LAZULI ✦

Lapis lazuli is a beautiful opaque stone of a rich and deep blue. It is always cut with a smooth or rounded form; faceting does not enhance it. The stone's smooth polish shows a rather waxy gloss. Although flecks of pyrite, which add a glint, are visible in some lapis, they do not add any degree of glitter or sparkle. Lapis lazuli is found in Russia and in the southern part of Asia. It was a product of ancient Babylonia and with malachite was highly esteemed by the early Egyptian civilization.

It is believed today that many ancient references to "saphiris" actually meant lapis, for the stone in so many instances was described as containing gold specks—a property of lapis lazuli but not of the sapphire. Today modern technology and scientific data have made it possible accurately to determine a stone's proper category.

Like malachite, lapis has served as an ingredient in the painter's art. The stones were powdered and mixed with an oil to produce a lasting paint, one which has retained its original color through the years. In the case of lapis lazuli, it is ultramarine blue; with malachite, a rich green.

Because lapis is a dense and opaque stone, it is not difficult to interpret in a flower arrangement. The deep blue of iris or clustered plumbago are possibilities for a likeness to lapis lazuli. A brown-stemmed branch would be an attractive element, not only for the pleasing line pattern, texture, and color variety it affords, but also for a suggestion of the brownish color of the matrix where the flecks of pyrite are embedded.

As for a container, none would be more appropriate than a cloisonné vase, especially one on which a quantity of powdered lapis lazuli is part of the surface decoration.

I think of malachite as the sanseveria of the mineral world. It is a fascinating stone, arresting the eye with its strength of alternating light and dark green stripes and its heaviness of texture. A soft stone, it breaks, chips, and cuts easily. Like so many stones, malachite has been known for centuries. Mined in ancient Egypt in 4000 B.C., it has long been used for ornamental purposes. Since it is found in fairly large pieces, many large and varied objets d'art are carved from it—vases, candlesticks, boxes.

Powdered malachite has been one of the important ingredients used in oil paints. Many of the old masters, Rembrandt, Titian, Botticelli, and Vermeer for instance, used this particular coloring in their oils. Malachite gave green its deep, opaque color. In this form it also has been responsible for the lasting qualities of much of the old masters' works; there has been little change in the paint's color value over the centuries.

I can think of no plant material better suited for an interpretation of this stone than sanseveria, the leaves of which are long, thick, smoothly textured, and richly striated, for malachite too is of similar striped appearance. The stripes may be light green alternating with darker green, and the stone is found with both wavy and straight lines. Sanseveria is a perfect duplication of this characteristic, with alternating light and dark lines in wide and narrow stripes.

28. MALACHITE. The circular pattern on this butterfly exemplifies a rare type of this stone, which is most often found with straight lines.

29. MALACHITE COMPOSITION. This modern design represents the link between malachite and the painter's art, since oil paints are still made using a powdered form of this stone. An abstract effect is created by cutting the tops and aligning the sanseveria leaves, by curving the flax into a directional design, and by forming a straight row of white daisies. The pestle, Oriental paint brushes, and pieces of malachite complete the interpretation.

30. MOONSTONE. The top stone is encircled by diamonds and set in a yellow-gold ring of simple but effective design, which allows the delicate coloring of the stone to show to advantage. The smoothly polished, unset stones show the soft, bluish light which distinguishes the moonstone.

✦ MOONSTONE ✦

A stone of mystery, the moonstone possesses a luminous and delicate opalescence within its depths. The stone's beauty is best seen by moving it slowly in natural daylight. The effect can be likened to that of moonlight moving over a body of water. The moonstone does not cut well and responds favorably only to a smooth polishing.

It is not surprising that this misty yet attractively glistening, faintly iridescent stone has stolen the hearts of men throughout the years. In India, for instance, it holds a place of such high regard that it is displayed only on yellow silk, a color revered by this Asian people.

Silky, ruffled, white petunia blooms are superior to all other plant material in the interpretation of the moonstone. Pale blue, a hue present in the play of opalescent coloring, suggests the possible inclusion of very light blue petunias or the palest blue morning-glories; the compatibility of texture and color in such combinations is excellent.

31. MOONSTONE COMPOSITION. A beautiful, large white clematis with a center composed of bellflowers was selected for this design. Small branches of baby's breath capture the moonstone's misty and elusive quality. The three polished moonstones in the right foreground look like drops of dew emanating from the single bellflower.

32. MOSS AGATE. These fernlike patterns are produced by minerals in liquid form which spread into the veins and fractures of the stone. (Courtesy of Ward's Natural Science Establishment, Rochester, New York and Monterey, California.)

✦ MOSS AGATE ✦

Moss agates have always been associated with superstition and ancient beliefs. It is no wonder, for it seems that nature uses the moss agate as a mirror to reflect the outlines of her trees, leaves, mosses, and clouds. Actually, what the viewer sees as he looks upon an agate depends upon his own imagination. The many varied and forceful patterns, an inherent characteristic, are caused by the infiltration of minerals through tiny cracks or seams in the stone. The agate itself may range from yellow to orange but more often is a slightly milky-white; the inclusions are seldom, if ever, any color but dark green, brown, or black.

Fairly large pieces are usually fashioned as paperweights or as objets d'art set in frames of metal. The smaller agates, outnumbering by far the larger pieces, are set as rings, earrings, and bracelets, or used as beads. Faceting or cutting into beads adds nothing to an agate's beauty, so it is usually cut flat, allowing the pattern of the inclusions to show through.

The leaves of white heather, the new growth of the astilbe, finely serrated branches of pfitzer juniper, finely cut leaves of the rose geranium, and many types of ferns are all excellent materials for interpretation. Combined they present a convincing likeness to moss agate. Intensely colored flowers are, of course, not appropriate, although stems of sweet alyssum with the flowers already gone to seed are an interesting and effective possibility.

It is not difficult to interpret the moss agate. I enjoy it most in a

▷ 33. MOSS AGATE ARRANGEMENT. Seen through an oval glass, the effect of this arrangement depicting moss agate is that of holding a polished stone up to the light, so that the lines and veins are clearly in evidence. Only conventional green foliage and flowers of pastel colors are used—blue agapanthus, pink centaurea, and white baby's breath, the latter for its delicate branching and elusive quality.

two-dimensional design to suggest the stone's natural inclusions. Any transparent substance such as glass or plastic, through which the flat design may be seen, is attractive. I would suggest the use of a large, convex glass from an old picture with a sheet of pink or beige plastic for the background. Against this, a pattern of lacy fern and moss give the effect of natural inclusions. You may prefer to simulate the stone itself by choosing a plastic sheet of yellow, milky-white, or grayish tone if available, but whatever your choice of color, plastic is texturally right in interpreting the moss agate.

✦ OBSIDIAN ✦

Obsidian is easily identifiable. Because of its textural quality, the eye has no trouble distinguishing it from black jet. The latter, a hard, coal-like mineral, is polished to a luster for a jeweler's use, whereas obsidian in itself is distinctly glassy and has a great reflective —not refractive—property. This brittle, hard black stone is volcanic glass, produced by intense heat and pressure.

An especially lovely variety is known as snowflake obsidian because of its white, flakelike inclusions in masses which spread and extend in many directions.

Many are the uses to which obsidian has been put over the thousands of years since it was first discovered. Being very sharp upon cleavage, it will cut and penetrate easily.

On the sides of a volcano in the Hawaiian Islands grows "sword plant," which is found nowhere else in the world. It is gray-green, and although it does not resemble obsidian in color, it is interesting to think of their similarities: both come from a volcanic environment and have sword-sharp edges.

▷ 34. OBSIDIAN AND JASPER COMPOSITION. The mood of an erupting volcano suggested by this abstract design was inspired by Sunset Crater, near Flagstaff, Arizona. The chunks of white spotted obsidian and red jasper, flame-colored gladiolas, and mullein of the hammerhead variety all symbolize volcanic activity. Because lava glints only slightly in sunlight, a base with a glinting effect, as though some small amount of silica were present, is used. The seed artichoke suggests dry vegetation. Since the flowers and mullein are seen as symbols rather than as plant materials, they are used abstractly. In fact it is the abstract character of the design that is responsible for its strong mood content.

90

The opal is a stone of irrepressible joy. In spite of the superstition of bad luck which it brings to mind, reaction to its beauty is one of delight. And who is immune? Colorists tell us that for complete satisfaction the eye must take in the spectrum, that is, see the basic primaries from which all other hues are made, or see hues which among them contain the basic primaries in their makeup. The coloring of an opal offers just that, for as we turn it slightly we see a ready-made rainbow of hues. A fire or flame opal is of special beauty, its body having an intense orange color, while flashes of other hues emanate from within. There are black opals, too; their flashes of light and color are even more intense because of the contrasting black.

Opals are found where once there was an inland sea. As the waters receded, minerals and rocks were exposed on the surface of the earth. Some, as they hardened, held minute quantities of sea water captured within them. It is where the liquid remains between the fissures or breaks in the stone that the bright and varied colors appear. As a prism breaks up light and reflects it in rainbow colors, so the fissures in the opal reflect light in a play of spectrum hues. Only recently have scientists been able to explain satisfactorily this marvelous display of colors. Unlike other gems and semiprecious stones, opals have never been successfully duplicated by man in his laboratory. There is no sparkle to the opal; rather it glows as though fire were burning within.

The omen of bad luck to the wearer of an opal that unfortunately surrounds this beautiful stone has two causes. We must blame the jewelers for one. Since the opal is a comparatively soft stone, it is easily chipped or broken. This has happened all too often as jewelers set the stone—a costly accident, to be sure, so the use of the opal was discouraged in the jeweler's trade. The second cause for the stone's disfavor stems from Sir Walter Scott's novel *Anne of Geierstein*. In the story, Anne and her mother were hounded by misfortune, supposedly because of their association with an opal. Perhaps only through personal experience will one rid himself of this fictitious omen.

Such an experience has been my lot. It came during college days when I spent a summer vacation as an employee in a jewelry store. One day a strong, pugilistic figure entered the shop. He asked to see some stones. Since he was vague as to what he wanted, I showed him variously set semiprecious stones. Nothing suited him until he spied a case of floating opals. These are chips or pieces of jagged stone in a tiny pear-shaped droplet of glass filled with pure glycerine and sealed. The thick liquid holds the opal chips in suspension, and they slowly move and turn about. In motion they glow and flash like many colored lights. The gentleman was fascinated; he purchased a chain with one of the floating opals swinging freely on it.

The following morning he returned anxious to see more opals, for his purchase had given him *good* luck, not bad! That very night he had been victor in a prize fight, defeating the contender for his world championship crown and thereby retaining his title. If Sir Walter Scott could write of this, he would certainly reverse the existing superstition that an opal means bad luck.

But opals possess an unfortunate characteristic—the tendency to dry out in time. When this happens, the flash and fire diminish. If the stones are not too old and have not flaked or chipped, glow and color can be restored by placing the stones for a week or so in a solution of half glycerine, half water.

Some of the most beautiful opals are found in Australia. Two famous opal-producing areas have fascinating names—Coober Pedy and Andamooka. These mines are generally known for their white opals, while the magnificent black opal comes from Lightning Ridge. Recently I visited a private museum in Alice Springs, in the center of Australia, and there on display was what I believe to be the most beautiful opal ever found. It is nearly drop-shaped, about the size of an almond, and has the quality of liquid gold shot through with intense flames, in which can be seen streaks of red, blue, yellow, violet, green, and orange—truly a magnificent gem!

Black opals seem to have an even more intensified coloration, because the flashes of vivid light are most pronounced against the black background. It has been said that black opals are becoming very rare, but I am hopeful that our wonderful earth will again yield more of these treasures. Mexico has produced many flame-colored stones, and it is entirely a matter of personal choice as to the desirability of one type of opal over another.

To interpret the opal, choose plant materials in clear hues with a minimum of red. If red is used, care must be exercised in the texture selected. The delicacy of poppies is the best choice, with individual florets of flame red gladiolas. Compatible with all this material and an excellent addition is the pink mimosa (Albizzia); its texture gives an effect of diffused pink as it appears in the stone.

The opal is not a stone of cold, formal elegance but a composite of qualities I would describe as warm, responsive, and altogether lovely. To depict the fire or flame opal, I know of nothing superior to the orange day lily (hemerocallis) with bright blue hydrangea, pink carnations, yellow daisies, and perhaps funkia leaves of a green and white variety.

36. BLACK OPAL. Intense colors are visible, each one changing to another hue as light strikes the stone's surface from a different direction. (Courtesy of the American Museum of Natural History, New York.)

37. THE HARLEQUIN PRINCE OPAL. Flashing blues and greens are seen in this famous opal, which is 215 carats in weight. Its clear and intense colors are strongly reminiscent of stained glass windows. (Courtesy of the American Museum of Natural History, New York.)

▷ 37. FLAME OPAL ARRANGEMENT. This design is a free and informal study of texture and color values. A smooth, orange glass container is used here with plant material to duplicate the varying colors of a flame opal. Tiger lily buds and open flowers of the trumpet vine are combined with yellow daisies, pink Albizzia, and a strange, variegated green-and-white leaf from the turquoise-berry vine, the latter suggesting the stone's irregular color play. Pink and red cosmos, blue lupine, and thin threads of pine needles combine to represent the fine lines of color which appear and disappear in the opal.

94

✦ ROSE QUARTZ ✦

Those who prefer pastel coloring to vivid hues will especially enjoy rose quartz, a stone with a pink, softly diffused color caused by tiny infractions within the body of the quartz. It is found generally in large forms of varied description: sometimes opaque, sometimes translucent, sometimes almost white showing just an overtone of pink. Occasionally, a fairly clear piece is found of a size suitable for carving into a figure, such as the elephant shown in this composition.

Rose quartz is a soft stone, so it can be carved without much effort; floral designs are popular motifs. Because it chips and cracks easily, this stone is not suitable set in jewelry subjected to hard wear. It is, however, used in bead form. A necklace of rose quartz combined with the lovely amethyst is an exquisite thing.

To interpret rose quartz characterized by diffused pink, it is easy to visualize a parallel in flowers of many small blooms: the snapdragon, with its small flowers borne in terminal racemes; the astilbe, with its tiny flowers profusely carried in spirelike clusters; and flowers with tiny threadlike petals, such as the *Sedum spectabile* or the pink centaurea with its fringelike petals.

Pink asters also are a good choice; their fine petals make them compatible. To interpret rose quartz with little or no pattern marked by diffusion, the smooth-petaled lycoris lily is excellent in form as well as texture.

▷ 38. ROSE QUARTZ COMPOSITION. The heavy marble base supports a large piece of rose quartz in the shape of a wedge, which allows plant material to be placed behind it. Since this particular stone is Vermont quartz, a rock of heavy crystalline content, the pink *Sedum spectabile* with its finely cut flowers is most compatible with it. Pink lycoris lilies echo the color and texture of the highly polished elephant, which contrasts dramatically with the large, rough stone. Deep pink verbena with tiny white hearts and small petals present a pleasing color accent. The green foliage provides contrast in hue, and the feathery evergreen, chamaecyparis, supplies height to balance the apparent weight of the stone.

39. SARDONYX AND CAMEO. The sardonyx piece at the right shows the alternating white and colored bands which characterize this stone. At the left is a cameo, illustrating a use which jeweler-artists have traditionally made of this stone's two-color effect.

✦ SARDONYX ✦

Sardonyx is a variety of onyx made up of alternating layers of sard (a very hard, deep orange-red variety of chalcedony, also called carnelian) and a white chalcedony quartz having a waxlike luster. A very old stone, sardonyx was known to the ancients; it was one of the first stones used in glyptic art. The mineral content prevents this stone from adhering to wax, so it was a favorite substance for use as seals and for making imprints on clay tablets.

Because of the formation of sardonyx in layers varying in darkness from white to black, artist-jewelers for centuries have used this stone for carving scarabs and cameos, which were especially popular during the Victorian period. The beauty of sardonyx is best brought out in cameos, which allow the colored background of the stone to set off the design carved from the lighter layers above. Incidentally, it was sardonyx from which the cameo of "Victory," described in the account of topaz (page 102) was fashioned. The figurine and chariot were carved in the white layers so that they were raised on a background of soft reddish pink.

Sometimes the striated onyx (stripes of white and black) are carved in reverse, that is, in intaglio. In this type of work the figure is engraved *below* the surface of the stone. Perhaps one could liken this to the arrangement of a stage setting, the figures taking position within the frame of the stage, the flat top (from which the design recedes) representing the plane of the curtain.

In thinking of cameos, the delicately colored pink-and-white seashells called "shell cameos" come to mind. These are quite beautiful but of course are not stones. Although carving shell cameos is the work of artist-craftsmen in a number of countries, it is an especially large industry in Italy.

The most beautiful rendition in plant material to suggest carved sardonyx (and shells) is achieved with the aquilegia of a variety which has a corolla of deep, almost maroon petals curved inward with white petals around it. I know of nothing better suited to the interpretation of cameo than this form. Its color is excellent too, for it matches the most prized of cameo colors—a deep maroon background with lighter color above. The leaves of the aquilegia lend themselves well too, for in pattern they give the illusion of a carving.

White camellias are a good choice, as are those of shell-pink color. The thick and heavy texture of gardenia, magnolia, and rose is also appropriate for interpretation.

Shell cameos and those carved from sardonyx often have a yellowish cast. For this reason, flesh-colored roses or richly textured flowers are a good choice. However, scale must be considered here, as cameos are usually quite small. Carvings on larger shells are found, and in this relation an interpretation using larger flowers is appropriate.

99

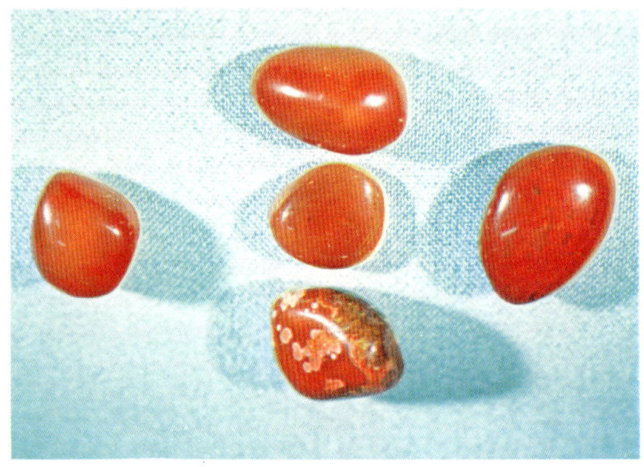

40. CARNELIAN. These deep reddish orange stones belonging to the sardonyx group are polished by what is known as the tumbling method.

▷ 41. CARNELIAN ARRANGEMENT. Because of this stone's long history, an old, almost primitive, pottery vase with a burned antique finish was selected for this design; it suggests a type of jar found in Persia. Bronze-flame-colored gladiolas depict the vivid color of carnelian. (Flame-colored zinnias may also be used in an interpretation of this stone.)

According to Pliny, topaz was first found on a misty and fog-cloaked island in the Red Sea to which mariners had difficulty finding their way. Since the island was called Topaza, a Greek word meaning "to guess or seek," it was natural that the lovely quartz discovered there would be named topaz. Today topaz is found in many areas, although the Oriental topaz is still greatly sought.

There are a number of shadings and variations in the makeup of topaz, but the most valuable is the deep, rich brown color. In cutting, this stone is always faceted since it would lack sparkle and brilliance otherwise. My preference is the lighter golden topaz; it has the lively color of sparkling champagne.

For a long time it was believed that the ancients never engraved Oriental topaz. An old book, however, mentions a topaz of 29 carats on which was engraved in Arabic, "No one accomplishes but God." In the Generosio Collection in Turin, there is a topaz carved in intaglio to represent Victory enthroned on a chariot.

I prize a beautiful copy of this topaz. The story behind it begins in Florence around 1900, when a box of precious and semiprecious stones was sold to a buyer from Naples. This exquisitely carved pink-and-white stone cameo was among the contents. Because it was a model from which craftsmen in Pompeii copied the design in shell cameos, the shop owner was reluctant to sell it. Recognizing the subject, I was determined to purchase this lovely piece. Since my Italian was *non 'est,* my only recourse was sign language, with help from a few sympathetic bystanders. I am sure the shopkeeper's black eyes and my blue ones struck many sparks during an hour of frustration and pleading. However my refusal to budge paid off: I left the shop as owner of the cameo "Victory," not enthroned on a chariot, but as thrilled and happy as could be.

▷ 42. TOPAZ AND AMBER COMPOSITION. Since the sparkle of topaz is difficult if not impossible to achieve with plant materials, the stone's association with the autumn season—it is the birthstone for November—was chosen as the theme of this composition. Trees and plants turn russet, orange, and gold in fall; therefore, dried plant materials such as yellow artichokes gone to seed, fern fronds with dark brown seed pods, leaves in soft beige and tan, and rust-colored chrysanthemums are used. The tallest stem of dried fishtail palm wins a place in this interpretation for its suggestion of the sea, the source of amber, while the spoon cactus represents the smooth, waxy texture of opaque amber. A base of myrtlewood indigenous to the Holy Land is used.

In the days of Abraham, turquoise was mined in the Sinai Peninsula. Large quantities were taken from the earth from 5300 until 1000 B.C. Then for nearly 3,000 years the mines were unworked; in fact they were entirely forgotten. In 1845 these mines of Abraham and Isaac were reopened, but although some stone is taken out today, the amount is nothing compared to that mined during the early centuries.

Pliny in his writings described the color of turquoise as sky blue. Indeed, the most beautiful stones are a sky blue with a slight touch of green. The matrix adds a considerable character to turquoise. Matrix patterns in the turquoise found in Persia are of especially interesting design. Although the color of some of the stones found in Mexico and the western United States rivals that of Persian turquoise, in general the matrix is of less interesting pattern. Also there is a quality of dustiness about the American variety, and in color the stone is slightly more green than blue.

Turquoise is a soft stone, easily pulverized. For this reason it cannot be polished with the usual abrasive substance which would quickly wear away the stone. A smooth, soft gloss allowing the beauty of the matrix to show through is achieved by polishing with felt or leather. Softness renders the stone absorptive; greasy water or strong liquids penetrate the stone and affect the color, either fading it or making it darker.

An interesting fact related to turquoise is this: the Indians of Arizona, New Mexico, and South America, the Persians, and the Turks, who are all renowned as horsemen, had the common belief that if turquoise were worn it would protect them from injury should they fall from their horses. The Turks customarily attached

▷ 43. TURQUOISE COMPOSITION. The turquoise-colored ceramic stallion was the inspiration for this interpretive design because of this stone's traditional good luck association with the horse; thus pieces of polished turquoise are fastened to bridle and saddle. Skeletonized leaves of opuntia and dried cactus branches are used to suggest a desert mood. Light blue hydrangeas represent the broken textural effect of the stone. A brown branch of interesting line and a few light greenish blue larkspur lend height to the composition, which is completed by the rough pieces of freshly mined turquoise in the foreground.

turquoise stones to the bridles of their mounts to prevent injury should they be thrown. I wonder if this superstition is still believed by these people; if not, is it only habit or custom which dictates the prevalent use of turquoise on both horse and rider today?

Turquoise berries, from the vine of the same name, or the fruit of the turquoise berry tree are a good choice for interpretation. I have one such tree; although it is literally powdered with tiny white blossoms in May, the birds, especially the robins and cedar waxwings, unfortunately leave few berries on the branches.

There is a light, bluish green hydrangea which, if carefully trimmed to allow the brownish stems to show, will be a good representation of turquoise. A weed which grows profusely along the roadside in July called "chicory" is a good blue, if tempered by some green leaves. Also you can see turquoise in the blue-green of the light blue larkspur. The eye will blend the blue of the larkspur with the green of the foliage if used in correct proportions, and the spurs or "tails" of the larkspur, which are of a light greenish blue tint, are delightful in combination. Spanish bluebell or wood hyacinth is also a good choice. In the spring of the year, muscari gives an excellent interpretation; it suggests little beads of turquoise.

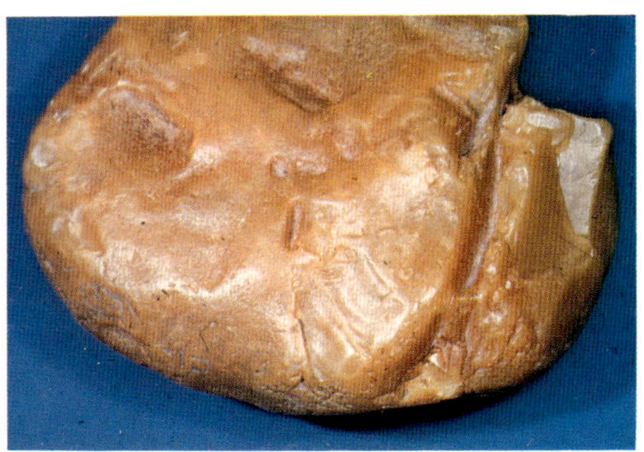

44. AMBER. This light golden substance is smooth and rich in texture. (Courtesy of Ward's Natural Science Establishment, Rochester, New York and Monterey, California.)

3. *STONES OF ANIMAL & VEGETABLE ORIGIN*

✦ AMBER ✦

Amber, the "sunshine stone," like coral, ivory, and pearls, is not classified as an inorganic mineral because it was once part of a living organism. Amber is actually a fossilized resin from pine trees, buried by ocean water thousands of years ago. It has been known to man since he began his trek across Europe from the Baltic to the Adriatic Sea. Amber found its way from the Baltic to the Mediterranean and then, by way of the Oriental trade routes, to the Far East. Because of its light weight and the ease with which it could be carried, it served as an excellent medium of exchange. It was also greatly desired by southern Europeans because of its beauty.

To pagan man this opaque yellow-toned solid washed up from the sea was "imprisoned sunshine." Sicilian amber has the beautiful color of dark sherry wine, while that from Burma (carved in China and called Chinese amber) is an orange-red color. Both of these ambers are clear and transparent.

As the resin from pine trees flowed, flies, ants, and small insects were trapped in the gummy substance, and when it solidified, it held the little insects entombed forever within its golden depths. These particular pieces of amber containing insects were greatly sought and prized during the Victorian era.

If amber is heated, it gives off an aromatic odor; if rubbed by a piece of wool, it becomes electrified and will draw bits of dust, lint and paper toward it. The Greeks called amber *elektron,* and the Latin *electrum* is the word from which our term "electricity" comes.

Coral, a product from the tropical seas, is a hard substance composed of the skeletons of millions of tiny marine animals (polyps) which live closely together in large colonies attached to any type of lime deposit or sandhill. They grow into what is known as "tree colonies" with branches; the white variety especially looks like very small flowers. It is interesting that these "flowers" are a means of protection for the tiny sea creatures. As an enemy approaches, they fold up their tiny, starlike petals and become motionless to make themselves less easily detected. Because of the coral's plantlike form, the reefs, shelves, and atolls where they are found have been described as "gardens of the sea."

Many varieties of coral abound, differing in shape, color, and form. An interesting "pipe organ" variety is interpreted in the composition shown. Not all can be used in jewelry, but those which are take a polish which has an almost porcelainlike surface. The finished product is never iridescent but has a satinlike gleam.

A light orange-pink type, known as branch coral, is of value when made into jewelry of a different style. Its tiny, fairly smooth branches are easily drilled and are especially interesting when strung as necklaces or bracelets. Much jewelry is made of oxblood coral in and around Italy. The greatest source for this deeper red coral is the Mediterranean, although it is gathered elsewhere in smaller quantities. A lovely whitish coral with splotches of pink or yellow is large and heavy enough to be cut into beads.

Coral has enjoyed popularity in cycles. As fashion dictates, demands for coral rise and fall. It enjoyed great popularity during the Victorian era, when pins, earrings, and necklaces were set with coral in combination with pearls. Frequently colored enamels were employed to enhance the beauty of these settings.

Even though coral is brittle and breaks easily, this product, loosely classified as a semiprecious stone, has been used for centuries in India for decorative objects such as vases, trinket boxes, cases, tables,

▷ 45. CORAL COMPOSITION. This design was inspired by the "pipe organ" coral, around which it is composed. Tritoma was chosen because of the similarity between the formation of its petals and the short, pipelike segments of the coral's strange growth pattern. Red dahlias further the color effect and provide textural contrast. Papyrus is arranged so that the shadows on the background suggest the movement of sea water around the coral formation. (Plant material similar to papyrus could also be used to achieve this effect of movement.) The clustered seed head of jack-in-the-pulpit adds textural interest, and the red berries duplicate the appearance of oxblood coral beads.

and other objets d'art. In Tibet, a land far from the source of coral, it is a very much treasured ornamentation combined with lapis lazuli (red and blue seem to be a universally favored color combination) and often with pearls.

It is relatively easy to establish associative interest when interpreting coral through plant material. For instance, oxblood coral may be likened in texture and color to the tall red canna lily, which grows so profusely in India, where coral has great popularity. Poppies have a color similar to that of oxblood coral too, and there are other poppies which match the white and pink corals.

Off the shores of the Hawaiian Islands (purportedly the only source in the world) there grows a black coral which is found deep in the ocean. Divers wrest it from its place of growth and bring "trees," actually bushes two or three feet in height, up to the surface. From this type of growth, black coral jewelry is carved in the form of pendants, rings, beads, and as insets in bracelets. This variety of coral may be interpreted by using a small bush with dried branches. The branches should be carefully pruned so as to be of good design—all leaves should be removed—and they should be allowed to dry until they become quite dark, then sprayed with black paint.

In Taiwan there are various carvings using a beautiful orange-red coral. These are of flowers, fruits, or figurines and are often as much as eighteen inches high. Because this coral is often found in curved growths, skilled craftsmen usually carve figurines leaning or somewhat bending, following the natural lines. Many examples of these carvings are also found in Japan, where designs are executed with great skill.

Many tropical flowers are of this clear orange-red color; hibiscus is one, and the African tulip is another. Ixora is a good likeness, since its small flowers remind one of beads. There are many berries and seeds found in this color, which increases the range of interpretive possibilities. There is a gorgeous tea rose of magnificent satin-sheen which is a perfect likeness in both color and texture to the coral of this particular variety.

When interpreting this coral, remember to use a minimum of green plant material. Color used as background may introduce a feeling of the sea and will complete the effect of a well-planned and studied composition.

✦ IVORY ✦

Ivory is a white, hard, closely knit tissue forming the tusks of elephants, walruses, etc. The best ivory is elephant ivory from Equatorial Africa; it is very finely grained (although the grain is visible), and very smooth to the touch. Young ivory is the softest and can be cut more easily than older tusks.

Ivory has been appreciated by mankind through the ages; three to four thousand years before the time of Christ it was used for barter. Artists have carved ivory with a remarkable degree of perfection and with incredible three-dimensional effects: circles within circles, balls within balls, and so on. Examples of the most delicate carvings from the past exist today; their appeal and soft, creamy white beauty are unquestioned. The Chinese excelled at carving ivory, and there are many fine examples which have been carved in India and Japan. The art is practiced today in all of these areas, and works of great intricacy and skill are still being produced.

"Scrimshaw" is a term given to the carving of the teeth of the sperm whale. Although many whales are toothless, the sperm whale has huge teeth, which were the medium for much of the carving done on whaling vessels. Many museums have carved ivory among their treasures. I urge you to see them; linger to study the remarkable designs and especially the scenes depicted.

In my own collection I treasure an intricately carved antique ivory box. On examining design details, one can read a story. I call it "Invitation to Tea." There are recognizable trees (mimosa, palm, wisteria) growing in an Oriental garden which shelters a summer house. In that house, on a balcony reached by a few oblique steps, sits a figure with a fan in hand. He is about to enjoy a cup of tea, for a cup rests on the table before him. The carving of these tiny but discernible objects holds great fascination for me. Imagine my delight upon opening the box to find a square of ivory, sliced very thin, with delicate calligraphic characters on one side! Could this have been a calling card in a box intended to hold them? I wonder.

Richly textured flowers such as the creamy rose, magnolia, and white wisteria have a sheen and luster which are reminiscent of ivory, as are the tulip and tuberose.

▷ 46. IVORY COMPOSITION. Calla lilies, chrysanthemums, and mitsumata are used here to create a design embodying the clean sculptured lines and textural quality of carved ivory. A section of uncarved elephant tusk is used as a base for two netsuke. The pièce de résistance, however, is the large white chrysanthemum lying obliquely at the left, which carries the eye from the tall line to the edge of the composition: this is a carved ivory flower, a perfect example of nature's influence on the artist.

The softly glowing beauty of pearls entitles them to the term "precious." Although they are not of mineral origin like the precious stones, they are greatly desired and exert a strong fascination on all who see them. There are many who consider pearls to be the perfect and unadulterated gift of nature. Pearls have been sought for centuries for use as personal adornment and were included in the treasuries of all the old civilizations. In Far Eastern countries, rulers and the families of the wealthy have kept the finest in their collections. Often they were stored in most unusual places within the household —in tips of old slippers, cracked wooden boxes, old rags, and even inside rafters. When visitors came, the pearls were brought out to be shown. The poorest quality was displayed first; then, after days of waiting, the best were proudly shown. Seldom did a family wish to part with its treasures, but when this was necessary, the collection of precious stones was sold before the pearls.

The pearl's high place in the world of gems parallels that of the lotus in the world of plants and flowers. There is much similarity in their origins, environment, and in their color and texture. Both are products of watery sites, the lotus springing from the muddy depths of a pond or pool and the pearl from the depths of the sea. The purity of color in a lotus, its sheen, iridescence, and delicacy of texture are phenomenally like a rosée pearl of the finest quality and color.

The finest pearls are called Oriental and have been found for centuries near Bahrein in the Persian Gulf. The best are called "first Orient." There are nine grades of pearls, each having a name designating its color or luster. The poorest quality is Astra; the finest is Venus.

Cultured pearls need no introduction, as they are very well known and within the reach of everyone. They are grown in a mollusk, as is the Oriental pearl; however, with the cultured pearl the hand of man intervenes and places an irritant in the mollusk. A tiny bead, cut from the nacre of another shell, is placed inside the mantle of the mollusk, and following the rule of nature the irritant is slowly covered with nacre which, being the color of the inside of the shell, becomes a pearl of that tint.

A delicate blush pink—almost white, yet possessing all the radiance of diffused spectrum colors—is the finest color in a pearl. Often only a person who has handled pearls a great deal can distinguish Oriental from cultured pearls, and sometimes even he cannot be certain until scientific tests are made.

Rosée pearls are a delicate, creamy pink. Their texture is rich and lustrous, imparting a warm, lifelike quality. There is something compelling about genuine pearls; to experience this, hold a necklace between thumb and index finger and let it hang along the inside of the wrist, showing its lustrous beauty and color. This method of examining pearls is also a good way to determine whether the color is right for the complexion of the wearer. Unlike gem stones, pearls must harmonize with the skin tones of the woman who will wear them.

Black pearls are likened in an old Chinese description to "frosted bronze," or the "hesitant shimmer of gun metal." They have an iridescent quality just as the white pearl has, but the body is dark gray. Despite their rarity, black pearls do not have as wide an appeal as white pearls.

Baroque pearls, imperfect in shape and form, have grown into many interesting and unusual shapes and have been employed as the bodies, heads, or other parts of figures in jewelry.

Legends abound regarding pearls, their lure, and the women or men who wore them. Cleopatra made history with a pearl, and Queen Elizabeth I became the epitome of fashion by wearing pearls in multitudinous quantities. Other ladies of note have coveted pearls too and have worn them in every conceivable way. During the Byzantine period in Italy, women over forty were forbidden to wear pearls, but such was the lure of this jewel that they could not be stopped, and although taxed they still wore them.

A volume called the *Book of the Pearl* contains a wealth of information and legend. One account tells how they are sold in open markets in Bombay. When a buyer sees pearls he is interested in he sits down with the merchant, and with a cloth spread over their laps they carry on their bargaining by means of finger and thumb pressure until they arrive at a satisfactory amount. In this way, no one other than the two principals knows the price paid. This method has been employed elsewhere for the sale of gems other than pearls, depending on the custom of the area and the value involved.

Early in the 14th century the Chinese cut tiny figures of Buddha and inserted them in mollusks. Thus they were the first to attempt to produce cultured pearls. However, they did not continue this practice, and it became only a fact of history. Also in this century the Chinese conceived the idea of making pearls. The method is fantastic and is explained in a communication from Peking as follows:

"In a basin half full of water, place the largest mussels to be found. Set in secluded place—so the dew may fall thereon, but where no female approaches—neither the barking of dogs nor crowing of chickens to be heard.

"Pulverize some seed pearls (yo tchu) as are used for medicine. Moisten this powder with juice expressed from leaves of species holly (Che ta-kong lao) then roll into perfectly round pellets size of a pea. Permit these to dry under moderate sun—carefully insert in shells of mollusks. Each day for 100 days nourish mussels with equal parts of powdered ginseng, china root, peki—a root more glutinous than isinglass. Combine all with honey and mold in form of rice grains."

Quite a detailed formula, but it omitted telling how to open the shells or explaining the importance of seclusion from women, dogs, and chickens.

An amusing story is told about a well-known actress who gave a garden party to which some of her so-called best friends were invited. She wore a magnificent rope of pearls. While talking to her guests, one lady asked, in a caustic manner, if the pearls were genuine. The reply of the hostess was quick and proof of her sharp wit: "They are real, but you need your *own* teeth to prove it."

The "bite test" is a reliable one to determine if pearls are genuine. A real pearl, whether Oriental or cultured, will feel like a stone if tested between the teeth. Just rubbing one against the front of the teeth will give the same effect. (However, as the heroine of the story above remarked, the teeth must be your own!) Imitation pearls have a very smooth, unmistakably waxlike feel against the teeth. In my lectures it is always amusing, and the audience joins in gaily, when I ask them to test any pearls they are wearing in this way.

On a television program one evening, there appeared a Japanese gentleman whose profession the panel had to guess. After the introduction of Mr. Casey, whose claim to fame was his having found the world's largest pearl, it was announced that he would appear with this huge gem in a department store the next day. I made a point of going to see it, and two things stand out in my memory.

47. PEARL ARRANGEMENT. Sea-fan coral was chosen as a background and a shallow mushroom coral as the container for this design depicting the natural environment of the pearl. A piece of mirror forms the base; water, to suggest a small wave, is allowed to spread over its surface. Water lilies of various hues are combined with the heavily ribbed leaves of sea lettuce, which have a deep shadowy effect. The stems of carnations with a few curling leaves are suggestive of underwater vegetation.

First, this pearl, which I had expected to see displayed among elegant velvets and satins, to my dismay was in the electric appliance department among toasters, frying pans, and percolators! The setting was incongruous and perhaps colored my perception and appreciation. The pearl itself was irregular in shape and about the size of a half-dollar; it was rather flat, with an imperfect, flawed surface. To me it looked gross. I could not help but think of the dainty miniature arrangements often found in flower shows: they are exquisite and delightful, but when they exceed a certain size (approximately three inches) they are no longer dainty and gemlike in quality and have lost their appeal. The same was true of this pearl: it was misshappen and had become too large to be considered a dainty gem.

Genuine pearls should be worn as often as possible, since the moisture and warmth of the human body are what keep them lustrous and "alive." If not worn for a number of years they tend to dry out, flake, and become dull. Is this not proof of the need for all things created by God to be sustained by the warmth of love?

48. PEARL AND SHELL COMPOSITION. The large iridescent shell has the textural quality of the finest rosée pearls. Sand dollars, little shell domes, and sea-lettuce coral in the foreground suggest the pearl's home as well as providing an interesting contrast of texture. Pale green water plants combine with the snowberry, similar to the pearl in form, and darker, green-ribbed leaves of sea lettuce are placed on the left side. Choice miniature cyclamen are clustered in the center.

APPENDIX: BIRTHSTONES & INTERPRETIVE PLANT MATERIALS

MONTH	STONE	PLANT MATERIALS
January	garnet	beebalm, carnation, dahlia.
February	amethyst	gloxinia, Parma violet, larkspur, delphinium, anemone, clematis, purple pansy.
March	bloodstone	red-veined croton, carnation, saxifrage.
April	diamond	pink rose, daisy, lupine, lilac, fern, artemisia.
May	emerald	magnolia leaf, saxifrage, ginger leaf, bells of Ireland, green Fuji chrysanthemum (for the lighter green stone).
June	pearl	lotus, datura lily, snowberry, water lily, sweet pea, magnolia, tulip, poppy (combined pastel colors).
July	ruby	red rose, cardinal flower, canna lily, dahlia, celosia.
August	sardonyx	aquilegia, columbine, peace rose.
September	sapphire	cornflower, lobelia, lupine, delphinium.
October	opal	orange marigold, wild aster, bells of Ireland, Queen Anne's lace, lupine, wild carrot, daisy, pink and yellow mimosa, cosmos, snapdragon.
November	topaz	bronze and gold chrysanthemum, marigold, autumn leaves, fern seed pods, dried plant material in brown, gold, and russet.
December	turquoise	blue-green hydrangea, lupine, delphinium, muscari, turquoise berry vine or tree.

BIBLIOGRAPHY

Briggs, Henry: *Encyclopedia of Gems,* Los Angeles, 1944
Church, A. H.: *Precious Stones,* London, 1908
Dieulafait, Louis: *Diamonds and Precious Stones,* Glasgow and London, 1874
Guebelin, Edward: *Precious Stones,* Berne, 1963
Gump, Richard: *Jade: Stone of Heaven,* Garden City, New York, 1962
Kessel, Joseph: *Mogok, the Valley of Rubies,* London, 1960
Kraus, Edward H. and Slawson, Chester B.: *Gems and Gem Materials,* New York, 1947
Kunz, George Frederick: *Curious Lore of Precious Stones,* New York, 1938
————and Stevenson, Charles H.: *Book of the Pearl,* New York, 1908
Oved, Sah: *The Book of Necklaces,* London, 1953
Seidler, Ned: *Gems and Jewelry,* New York, 1964
Verrill, A. Hyatt: *Minerals, Metals, and Gems,* New York, 1939
Weinstein, Michael: *The World of Jewel Stones,* New York, 1958
Zim, Herbert S. and Shaffer, Paul R.: *Rocks and Minerals,* New York, 1957

123